Commendations for *Student Ministry by the Book*

"*Student Ministry by the Book* is one of the most powerful, compelling, and needed books written for those who care deeply about students and student ministry. Ed Newton and Scott Pace have created a triple threat resource that is rich in theology, highly personal in its practicality, and conversational in its tone. Furthermore, this is a book that is just as beneficial to a parent as it is to a youth pastor. I can't wait to give copies to the student ministry team at our church!"

—*Brent Crowe, vice president, Student Leadership University*

"One of the things I have always loved about Ed and Scott is that they preach and teach by the Book. Now they have collaborated to give us a new fantastic resource in *Student Ministry by the Book*. You and your ministry will be encouraged and equipped with this much needed biblical philosophy and practical guide for youth ministry."

—*J. Roger Davis, president, YM360*

"In *Student Ministry by the Book*, Scott Pace and Ed Newton have given clear, concise, and biblical guidelines for understanding students and building the foundations for excellent youth ministry. I know these men well, and this book is an authentic reflection of their heart for students and student leaders. If you are a youth pastor who is just "trying to figure it out," you need this book. If you want to be more than an activities director and begin to build student disciples, this is the place to start."

—*Andy Harrison, student ministries specialist and Falls Creek program director,*
Baptist General Convention of Oklahoma

"The students in your ministry will touch a day we will never see. Therefore, impacting this generation with the gospel should be the heartbeat of anyone who serves in student ministry. What you hold in your hands is an excellent tool based on biblical principles to help you make that impact! Ed and Scott's wisdom and experience in pointing students to Jesus will educate your mind, encourage your heart, as well as strengthen your mission. This book is written with passion and practicality. Read it, re-read it, and apply it! You and your ministry will be blessed because of it!"

—*Zac Hufty, minister of campus development, Houston's First Baptist Church,*
Houston, TX

"My friends Ed Newton and Scott Pace have written a much needed book. I love the balance they strike—the chapters recognize that even though our culture has separated adolescents from adults in so many venues, they should be challenged with biblical and theological truths. In the two decades that I taught youth ministry, and now even more as a pastor, I sense a need to say things that matter—beyond keeping students entertained. The authors emphasize that students should be taught not only what to think but how to think. In a culture that floods every inbox, screen, and brain cell with information, learning how to recognize God's truth as distinct from that of the newsfeed is an urgent message. The church still has a role to play, partnering student ministry with parents to give teenagers the best chance for success in college and beyond. Well done, friends!"

"I enthusiastically recommend *Student Ministry by the Book* to every youth pastor and person preparing to be one. Ed Newton and Scott Pace have crafted a book that blends scriptural principles, cultural understanding, and current research. Both their overarching strategy and their practical applications are spot-on. The section on teaching teenagers the classic doctrines is worth the price of the book. This one belongs in your library."

"I am thrilled that *Student Ministry by the Book* has been included in the Hobbs College Library. It is a needed resource from authors Ed Newton and Scott Pace who know student ministry from both an academic and practical perspective. I believe *Student Ministry by the Book* will be an influence on student pastors and student ministries in churches for years to come. Beyond that, I hope the heart of this book—that generations of teenagers would come to know the Lord and learn how to walk with him through his Word—is passed on to each person who reads it."

Commendations for Hobbs College Library

"This series honors a wonderful servant of Christ with a stellar lineup of contributors. What a gift to the body of Christ! My hope and prayer is that it will be widely read and used for the glory of God and the good of his Church."

—*Daniel L. Akin, president, Southeastern Baptist Theological Seminary*

"This series is a must have, go-to resource for everyone who is serious about Bible study, teaching, and preaching. The authors are committed to the authority of the Bible and the vitality of the local church. I am excited about the kingdom impact of this much needed resource."

—*Hance Dilbeck, executive director, Baptist General Convention of Oklahoma*

"I am very excited about the dynamic leadership of Dr. Heath Thomas and his vision of the Hobbs College Library at Oklahoma Baptist University that he is developing. Through his work as Dean of the Hobbs College of Theology, this 21-volume set of books will ascend the theological understanding of laypeople, church leaders, pastors, and bi-vocational pastors. Therefore, I want to encourage you to participate in this vision that will equip your church to make a greater difference for Jesus Christ in your community and around the world."

—*Ronnie Floyd, senior pastor, Cross Church, Northwest AR, and former president, the Southern Baptist Convention*

"This series offers an outstanding opportunity for leaders of all kind to strengthen their knowledge of God, his word, and the manner in which we should engage the culture around us. Do not miss this opportunity to grow as a disciple of Jesus and as a leader of his church."

—*Micah Fries, senior pastor, Brainerd Baptist Church, Chattanooga, TN*

"The Hobbs College Library is a perfect way to help people who want to grow in the basics of their faith. Whether you are a layperson or longtime pastor, this tool will help give you the theological base needed for ministry today. I highly recommend this tremendous resource to anyone wanting to deepen their understanding of Scripture."

—*Jack Graham, pastor, Prestonwood Baptist Church, North TX, and former president, the Southern Baptist Convention*

"The best resources are those that develop the church theologically while instructing her practically in the work of the Great Commission. Dr. Thomas has assembled an impressive host of contributors for a new set of resources that will equip leaders at all levels who want to leave a lasting impact for the gospel. Dr. Hobbs exemplified the pastor-leader-theologian, and it's inspiring to see a series put out in his name that so aptly embodies his ministry and calling."

—*J.D. Greear, pastor, The Summit Church, Raleigh-Durham, NC, and president, the Southern Baptist Convention*

STUDENT
MINISTRY
BY THE BOOK

STUDENT MINISTRY BY THE BOOK

*Biblical Foundations
of Student Ministry*

ED NEWTON *and* R. SCOTT PACE

HEATH A. THOMAS, *Editor*

OBU

B&H
ACADEMIC
NASHVILLE, TENNESSEE

Student Ministry by the Book
Copyright © 2019 Ed Newton and R. Scott Pace
Published by B&H Academic
Nashville, Tennessee

ISBN: 978-1-4627-9129-3

Dewey Decimal Classification: 251
Subject Heading: PREACHING \ PASTORAL THEOLOGY \ SERMONS

Printed in the United States of America
3 4 5 6 7 8 9 10 • 26 25 24 23 22
BP

To youth leaders,

the students they serve, and

for the raising up of a generation

that will reach the world for Christ!

Contents

Acknowledgments   *xiii*
About the Library   *xvii*

Part I. Defining Student Ministry   **1**
  1. Students' Identity in Our Culture   *3*
  2. Students' Identity in Christ   *17*
  3. Students' Identity in Our Churches   *35*

Part II. Designing a Student Ministry   **49**
  4. Relating to Students   *51*
  5. Reaching Families   *63*
  6. Recruiting Leaders   *79*

Part III. Discipling in Student Ministry   **93**
  7. Teaching Them to Walk   *95*
  8. Teaching Them to Think   *105*

  Conclusion: Final Thoughts and First Priorities   *125*
  Name and Subject Index   *129*
  Scripture Index   *131*

Acknowledgments

To a Savior that saved me, parents who raised me, mentors who invested in me, a wife who believed in me, children who blessed me, and a church who walks with me, I'm nothing without you!
—Dr. Ed Newton

I had the awesome privilege of growing up in a Christian home. We were the typical "every time the doors were open" church family, so youth ministry was a big part of my teenage years. I considered my youth pastor a personal friend. He was fun, exhibited godly character, and always made sure we had a great time. Many of my closest friends as a teenager were from our youth group, and I have countless stories of lock-in escapes, camp pranks, and general church mischief that we instigated. But, while these youth ministry memories are sentimental (and embarrassing!), they are also haunting. I was as involved as any student could have been, but I don't have any specific recollection of personal discipleship or spiritual growth that I could directly attribute to my youth ministry experience.

Sadly my testimony is not uncommon. To be fair, my attention during my teenage years was more focused on social interests than spiritual interests. But, at the same time, our success as student leaders must be measured by our faithfulness to cultivate a culture of discipleship and to provide opportunities for spiritual growth that has been largely absent in student ministries. While I regret the deficiencies of my youth ministry experience, God providentially used them as the impetus for my initial calling into student ministry, my passion to disciple teenagers, and my desire to see a youth ministry reformation of sorts. As a result, they also serve as the genesis for this book.

Ed and I first discussed partnering together on this project because we share this same burden for students and the ministries designed to reach them. He is a supremely gifted youth speaker because of his ability to convey solid biblical truth in a real, relevant, and relatable way for students. In addition, his personal experience as a youth pastor, combined with his investment in teenagers and partnerships with student ministries across the country, gives him a unique perspective that offers invaluable insights into current trends and contemporary needs in the world of youth ministry. I'm grateful for his friendship in life, his collaboration on this project, and his partnership in ministry for the sake of the gospel!

I am also thankful for others who have had a profound impact on my understanding of student ministry. The formal training I received from seminary professors like Ken Coley and others was invaluable and taught me the "ins and outs" of leading a student ministry. (They also entrusted me as a young youth pastor with their own children!) Other practitioners and student ministry leaders like Andy Harrison and Todd Sanders have also been influential in my ministry to students. Thanks, guys, for opportunities to serve with you and for the spiritual insights and practical skills you have modeled and shared along the way!

My passion for student ministry is also the result of the families and students I've had the privilege to serve through the years. I'm not sure I would have ever made it without the love, wisdom, and patient support of the Listers, Bowmans, Schofields, Mullaneys, Yarbers, Cramers, and Barbers! You were the "dream team" of parents! Of course, the students themselves have been the greatest reward.

I've watched God work in your lives and use you in ways beyond what we could have ever prayed or imagined. I'm honored to be a part of your story. "You are [my] glory and joy!" (1 Thess 2:19–20).

To the leadership of Oklahoma Baptist University and Southeastern Baptist Theological Seminary, thank you for your support and encouragement as you empower your faculty to expand our influence for the sake of Christ. To my colleagues at both institutions, you have been an inspiration, and you continually challenge me to grow as a scholar and a practitioner. In particular, to my friend and dean at OBU, Heath Thomas, thanks for your friendship, leadership, and for the privilege of contributing to this groundbreaking series. And, of course, thanks to the superb team at B&H Academic that makes writing such a joy!

Most of all, I'm grateful for my wife, Dana, who not only selflessly supported me in my years as a full-time youth pastor but has continuously encouraged and enabled me to invest in the next generation. As we've now entered into the world of raising our own teenagers, I'm grateful for how the Lord will use what we have learned through our years together in student ministry. I pray that our children—Gracelyn, Tyler, Tessa, and Cassie—will grow into faithful disciples through their teenage years. May God use them as part of a generation that ushers in his kingdom through humble obedience and devotion to Christ, and may we be faithful to teach them!

To my beloved Savior and exalted King, Jesus Christ, may you receive the honor and glory for any fruit born by this labor of love given as an offering to you!

—Scott Pace

About the Library

The Hobbs College Library equips Christians with tools for growing in the faith and for effective ministry. The library trains its readers in three major areas: Bible, theology, and ministry. The series originates from the Herschel H. Hobbs College of Theology and Ministry at Oklahoma Baptist University, where biblical, orthodox, and practical education lies at its core. Training the next generation was important for the great Baptist statesman Dr. Herschel H. Hobbs, and the Hobbs College that bears his name fosters that same vision.

The Hobbs College Library: Biblical. Orthodox. Practical.

PART I.

DEFINING STUDENT MINISTRY

CHAPTER 1

Students' Identity in Our Culture

A s the end of the semester approached, a young college student at a large secular university was sweating his grade in his most difficult course. So much was riding on his final exam—financial aid, athletic eligibility, social respect, and, on top of everything else, his parents' approval. He began to cram for the cumulative final, spending long hours attempting to learn a semester's worth of material in just a few short days. When the exam day finally arrived, he sat near the back of the class of 300-plus students and wrote feverishly for the entire two hours.

When the time expired, the professor instructed the students to put down their pens and turn in their papers. As students filled the aisles, placing their exams in a large stack on the professor's desk at the front of the classroom, the desperate student continued to write. After admonishing him several times, the professor finally threatened the student with a failing grade if he didn't stop and submit his exam. The student scribbled his last word and rushed to the front of the now empty classroom. His teacher informed him that there would be a letter-grade deduction for taking extra time. The student attempted to explain that he didn't have any margin for points off, but his pleas fell on deaf ears. With desperation in his voice, the student appealed to his parents' and his own notoriety, inquiring, "Do you know who my parents are? Don't you know who I am?!" The professor would not be strong-armed by some veiled threat and exclaimed in response, "I don't know who you are, who your parents are, or anything else about you! Turn in your exam!"

As soon as he realized his professor didn't know him or anything about him, the student quickly flipped halfway through the stack of exams, deftly slid his paper into the middle of the stack, and slammed them back down on the desk. After all, if the professor didn't know who he was, he wouldn't be able to distinguish from which exam he needed to dock points. The student smiled, wished his professor a great summer, and quickly escaped through the classroom door!

It's funny how we can benefit from our anonymity, like the student in the story. The student capitalized on the fact his professor didn't know him. But being anonymous also has a dark side when it comes to our identities. More and more in the modern world, students either don't know who they are deep within, or they attempt to *hide* their true identity from others. In either case they darken their hearts and deceive themselves.

God has a different plan. God made us to know ourselves, to know one another, and to be known—to live in the light and to live in love. By contrast, teenagers today too often are not known and not loved by others. They feel at war with themselves and others, morphing through biological changes while they ride an emotional roller coaster in the midst of a social hurricane. Often they feel like aliens in their own changing bodies and turbulent emotions. If biological changes and emotional volatility are not enough, they're beginning to consider their future aspirations and melting under the pressure of others' expectations. It's no wonder teenagers struggle with a basic question: Who am I?

Like symptoms of a deep sickness, the problem of not knowing oneself or being known by others expresses itself in intense and varied issues like suicide, confused sexual orientation, or gender dysphoria. But it actually manifests itself in more common examples like peer pressure, social acceptance, media preferences, habitual temptations, and personal behavior. The issue of identity impacts every aspect of a student's life!

Because of its foundational nature, student ministry must begin by helping teenagers understand their true identity and where it is found. But, in order to help them do this, we must first come to grips with the reality of who they are, who our world portrays them to be, and how God desires to work in the lives of students. Success in every job begins on the ground floor of knowing whom you're working with and what you're trying to accomplish. Student ministry is no different. Therefore, we must begin with understanding the truth about teenage identity.

Identity Confusion

In many ways our culture does not know how to define a teenager. There are so many different guidelines by which a student is measured. Obvious examples of this identity confusion abound. For instance, Hollywood determines the suitability of a film and restricts the age of its audience members based on subject matter, language, violence, and other content. Agencies recommend parental guidance (PG) for certain movies while other films stipulate a more specific line of demarcation such as PG-13. R-rated movies limit viewers based on their age and require them to be accompanied by a parent or guardian if they are not older than seventeen. Video games do the same thing, and their purchase is age restricted based on some of the same factors. However, there is not a specific standard to determine these criteria or the corresponding age restrictions, revealing the subjectivity at work in these regulations.

The subjectivity of our culture in regard to a teenager's identity is also recognized in a lack of consistency regarding privileges that pertain to being an adult. For example, note the differing age requirements for various activities our culture links with adult responsibility: obtaining a driver's license in order to operate a vehicle (16), military enlistment (18), employment (15), the purchase of tobacco products (18), voting rights (18), tattoos and body piercings (16), and the purchase of alcohol (21). Note as well the fact that the criminal justice system often categorizes sixteen-year-olds as "adult" offenders in major crimes. In all of these cases, except in the case of purchasing and consuming alcohol, adult responsibility is given in the age range that people normally associate with the teenage years. This variance between teenage and "adult" responsibility reflects a fundamental uncertainty in our culture regarding teenagers' identity and qualification as "adult."[1]

Some of the confusion stems from other forms of inconsistencies as well. Beyond the legalized age requirements, our culture seems to endorse "grown-up" behaviors in young teens like individual autonomy, social advocacy, and young entrepreneurship. But, at the same time, our society endorses "childish" behaviors in young adults that are irresponsible and immature. The concept of undefined adolescence has ultimately extended childhood by offering an excuse for naïve, reckless, and disobedient behavior.

---

[1] Some of these age restrictions may actually vary depending on the state, which only reinforces the point. Our culture is confused regarding the identity of teenagers and does not know how to classify them.

Regardless of where you may stand on these social issues, the absence of any specific demarcation of identity and responsibility clearly places teenagers in an undefined category. Adults have difficulty identifying teenagers, and teenagers have difficulty identifying themselves! The lack of objective criteria or defined expectations has resulted in widespread confusion throughout our culture regarding the identity of students. As a result, teenagers are left searching for something to define them and to help make sense of it all. Oftentimes they begin to claim an identity for themselves and devote their lives to living for a mirage that continually vanishes and never satisfies.

As youth leaders we cannot follow the blurred lines of how the world defines, and ultimately confuses, teenagers. Conforming to our culture's standards will only reinforce their lack of purpose and their license to live irresponsibly. This identity confusion, in the church and in our culture, has spawned an identity crisis among teenagers with monumental implications for us as student leaders.

KEY
∴ THESIS?

Identity Crisis

Considering our culture's uncertainty regarding teenagers during a life stage permeated with confusion, it's not surprising that students have no idea how to define their identity. As a result, they have become infected with what we call the "FALSE identity" syndrome. Both Christians and non-Christians suffer from it as students define themselves according to these five primary aspects of their lives. This acronym stands for:

- **F**riends
- **A**ttitude
- **L**ooks
- **S**kills
- **E**xperience

It is important that we grasp each of these so that we can help our teenagers and ourselves!

Friends

Perhaps the most common source of a misplaced identity among students is their peers. Teenagers often define themselves by who their friends are and how many they have. For example, if students are connected with the popular or cool crowd at school, then they naturally view themselves as significant. Likewise, if they feel disconnected from the more recognizable names and faces around school, then oftentimes they will view themselves as a loser or a loner. While the Bible teaches us that God does not show favoritism or define us by our relationships with others (Gal 2:6), students frequently determine their identity by their friends and typically go well beyond a self-assessment by association.

Oftentimes students will begin to allow their peer groups to define them in more practical and formative ways. Teenagers can begin to adopt the personalities, preferences, and values of their peer groups as their own. When they do, they begin to view their life through a stereotyped social lens. So the identity of their preferred school clique becomes the adopted image to which they conform. Everything from their musical interests to their worldview begins to be shaped by their particular peer group and its social reputation.

Another relational way students commonly define themselves is by their boyfriend or girlfriend. Sometimes a lack of love and acceptance at home facilitates a desperate need to be accepted by someone else. The emotional and physical affirmation a boyfriend or girlfriend offers can become the security blanket for a student that quickly develops into a form of social codependency. Beyond the infatuation they can have for their significant other, they can easily be deceived into viewing themselves based on their relationship status and their boyfriend or girlfriend's opinion of them.

There are also Christian versions of the friendship identity issue. Some of our students struggle to maintain their walk when they're not around their church friends. Others become conceited and self-righteous because of their close relationships with other believers. While some aspects of social influence and association are formative and healthy, teenagers can begin to rely on others' faith and spiritual interests as the basis for their own identity. Regardless of the type or number of friends they have, their social status is never their true identity.

Attitude

So much of the teenage years is characterized by hormonal volatility and the resulting emotional instability. In addition to their unpredictable moods, students are discovering their own personalities through social interaction while also being influenced by the prevailing attitudes of arrogance, indifference, and defiance in our culture. This combustible blend of ingredients often produces an attitude eruption that students adopt as their identity. A teenager's attitude can become a persona that begins to dominate their lives and dictate their behavior. While Scripture affirms the significance of our attitude (Phil 2:5), our emotional disposition is never intended to be the defining aspect of our identity.

The culture's influence on a teenager's attitude can be devastating. Our society's elevation of the socially elite can make students feel inferior and become psychologically secluded. This sense of inadequacy can cause them to retreat to an emotional hideaway that manifests itself in a reclusive or passive persona. Our culture also promotes a dismissive and apathetic disposition that "doesn't give a rip" as it disregards others and denies any sense of personal responsibility. This leads to an attitude of arrogance that resists authority and can develop into bullying behaviors.

Many teens today are also influenced by a sense of entitlement that believes they deserve—and therefore they demand—*everything*: from others' respect to unearned luxuries and economic or cultural opportunities. This privileged attitude degrades their peers and disrespects adults as they embrace their false identity and seize its destiny. Other students adopt an inflated ego as their identity based on our culture's principle that vulnerability and transparency reveal weaknesses that should not be exposed. But, because teenagers are experiencing so much inner turmoil, this persona becomes a façade that can cause them to emotionally implode.

Sadly, Christians can be guilty of some similar types of influences in our attempts to shape teenagers. For example, in our efforts to condemn the world and its unrighteous behavior, we may actually heap guilt and shame on our students who struggle with worldly habits or temptations. This may produce a withdrawn persona that begins to define them. Or, in our vigorous stance against sin, we can unintentionally promote an attitude of self-righteousness that encourages our teens to adopt an identity of superiority over others, although in a pious pharisaical guise. These spiritual personas are no different from the cultural attitudes; they are an image, not an identity. Our students must be rescued from the snare of defining themselves by their attitude.

Looks

We live in a shallow and superficial culture. An unhealthy emphasis on physical appearance and material possessions is nothing new. But, as part of the "selfie" generation, our students find themselves immersed in a world that is consumed with outward appearance. Technological advances like iPhones, laptops, and tablets as well as apps like Facebook, Instagram, Snapchat, and Twitter (among others!) feed a culture that prioritizes our egos, our appearances, and puts a premium on our looks. In light of this cultural force, it's not surprising then that so many of our teens get lured into the trap of defining themselves by their looks. Although this egocentric culture that evaluates others on the *outside* remains powerful, it stands in stark contrast to the biblical teaching that God evaluates us by the unseen person of the *heart* (1 Sam 16:7). Still, we must admit it is difficult for teens to see beyond their reflection in the mirror.

Students find their identity in their looks in a variety of ways. The most obvious factor is their physical appearance. Because of the drastic physical and biological changes teens experience, they commonly become self-conscious. Many of their struggles with self-perception stem from physical characteristics that a filter on an app can't change. Height, body type, skin color, or other personal features can foster some significant insecurities. Of course, those who fit the worldly picture of physical beauty aren't immune from this form of mistaken identity. In fact, they can be even more susceptible because they begin to define themselves by their superior good looks.

When students are not happy with their physical appearance, they may begin to change it as much as possible. Some become obsessed with working out and packing on the pounds, while others become consumed with starving themselves to shed them. Unhealthy extremes such as steroids, self-inflicted abuse, or eating disorders like anorexia or bulimia are all symptoms of a mistaken identity based on physical appearance. Some students attempt to distract people's attention away from their insecure physical features by expressing themselves with outrageous hair, body piercings, eccentric makeup, or other forms of appearance modification.

While they may not be able to substantially alter their physical body, students can manipulate other aspects of their looks to make themselves feel more comfortable or socially accepted. Style can become a defining element of their appearance as they begin to view themselves based on their fashion. This can be portrayed as "going for a certain look," when in reality it becomes a personified image. Teens begin to view themselves through the social lens people associate with the type of clothes they wear. Whether that's based on trendy brands and logos, styles particular with certain interests, or presenting themselves as "mature" through immodest and revealing apparel, students can mistakenly find their identity in their looks.

Skills

The teenage years can be a season of discovery as much as development. Students begin to discern their gifts and talents through their passions and interests. Their abilities can be multifaceted and can provide a sense of purpose. They can also discern their spiritual calling based on what God has gifted them to do. Those who struggle to identify any exceptional ability may begin to characterize themselves as less significant or even worthless. The Christian life is not about what we can do but what Christ has already done on our behalf and what he can accomplish through us (1 Cor 1:26–31; Phil 4:13).

A student's skill set develops into a limiting liability when they become consumed with their abilities and begin to define themselves by them. Their artistic, academic, or athletic capability, if left unguarded, can become an idol that is only exposed when their defining attributes are suddenly disabled. When an athlete is injured, a straight-A student bombs an exam, or an artistic submission or tryout fails, you'll often see students with misguided concepts of their identities completely unravel.

12

In addition, achievements in their areas of interests and talents can become the lens through which they view themselves. What they've accomplished, or what they haven't, can shape their image as a success or a failure. Accolades and adoration can artificially inflate teens' perspective of themselves while disappointments and failures can lead to personal disillusionment. These types of performance identity can also cause students to become egotistical, neurotic, or irrational in their behavior. But what students can or can't do does not define them.

Experience

Teenagers are frequently introduced to new experiences. Some of them are just initial opportunities to try something for the first time like playing for a school team or getting a job. Other times it's something they've waited for and anticipated, like driving a car or going on a senior high mission trip. New experiences can be some of the most formative aspects of their development, but they can't be misled into defining themselves by what they've done or haven't done. Sadly many teenagers are deceived into believing that their life experiences define who they are. But Scripture teaches us that our earthly accomplishments possess no eternal value and ultimately amount to a pile of worthless garbage (Phil 3:3–8).

This experiential form of mistaken identity can have some of the most devastating effects on teens. Many times the experiences they use to define themselves derive from curiosity, desires, or experimentation. Social drinking, pushing romantic boundaries, sexual encounters, and recreational drug use are commonly used to determine a student's identity. Some of the ugliest forms of bullying leverage this type of identity against teens with derogatory names associated with the experience. Students can even be labeled and derided for their lack of experience in these areas. So how far they have been on a date, whether they've ever drank or used drugs, and the illicit nature of what they've viewed or listened to all become experiential attributes that determine their identity.

Tragically, students can also identify themselves not by what they've done but by what's been done to them. Various forms of abuse can define students as victims or cause them to blame themselves for someone else's maliciousness. These wounds can become scars that haunt students with a disfigured perspective for the rest of their lives. These situations may not be easily discerned, but we must recognize that they are more common than we often acknowledge. We must provide students with a safe environment to dispel this mistaken identity and deliver them from its emotional bondage.

Other types of experiences can also lead to a misplaced identity. Students' upbringing can serve as their defining experience. Whether they come from a broken home or a traditional family, if they have overprotective parents or uninvolved parents, if their family is financially stable or financially struggling, or if they feel pressure to live up to their family's esteemed name or dysfunctional reputation, students' home life can naturally be misunderstood as their defining influence. But, regardless of the nature of their personal history or family situation, their past mistakes and failures, or their achievements and accolades, a student's identity is never defined by experience.

Conclusion

We have explored the powerful FALSE identities that mark the lives of teenagers (and maybe we've found that we have embraced one or more of them as well!). What we must understand is this: *a proper understanding of identity is critical, particularly in the context of student ministry.* Our culture's inability to accurately define a

This is what we build a ministry to Rising adults on!

teenager, combined with its influence on them to view themselves through false images and personas, leaves our students dazed and confused when it comes to this foundational truth. As a result, when our ministries fail to address the issue of identity, our attempts at spiritual depth and development ultimately become biblical "pep talks" that inspire virtues and values without ever penetrating their hearts and transforming their lives. Students can actually become more frustrated because their spiritual life and church involvement can develop into another masquerade that requires their best performance.

Therefore, we must be careful not to view students through these cultural lenses and reinforce their misplaced identities. Instead we must be diligent to help them understand where their true identity is found and how it impacts every aspect of their lives. This should be the ultimate goal of all of our ministry efforts: helping students find their identity in Christ. We can now turn our attention to a proper understanding of this truth and its implications.

CHAPTER 2

Students' Identity in Christ

The names Clark Kent, Peter Parker, Bruce Wayne, and Tony Stark are probably familiar to you. If they are, it's not because you recognize them as an outstanding newspaper reporter, the most popular student in school, or a wealthy tycoon. These four names are recognizable because of their secret identities—Superman, Spider-Man, Batman, and Iron Man! As superheroes, they fight for truth and justice and are able to accomplish the unthinkable. But, as their alter egos, they are ordinary people who are restrained by their stereotyped images and their average abilities.

The Bible is full of similar individuals, real people who were limited by their own insecurities, public perception, and character flaws. Although they weren't superheroes, when their true identities were revealed, they became spiritual heroes whom God used to accomplish his supernatural will! God used an ordinary shepherd to father the nations (Gen 12:1–3). He used a deceiver and doubter to form his covenant people (Gen 35:10–12). He used an everyday woman to become a judge of God's people (Judg 4). He used a shepherd boy to defeat a giant for his glory (1 Sam 17) and established him as the king whose descendant would be the King whose reign will never end (2 Sam 7:8–16)! He used a teenage girl to be the mother of the Savior of the world (Luke 1:26–38). The Lord chose a fisherman as his spokesman to convert 3,000 souls and give birth to the church (Acts 2:14–41). He confronted and converted a zealous Jew and appointed him as an apostle to the nations (Gal 2:11–16).

Perhaps even more remarkably, Jesus stripped off the social labels, disarmed the detractors, and healed the brokenness of the least, the last, and the lost. He liberated them and taught us that these superficial characteristics were not their identity; they were simply an image that kept people from recognizing who they truly were. For instance, Jesus dispelled the myth that a blind man's condition or his family defined him as a condemned sinner (John 9:3). He also didn't define the widow according to her undersized offering (Luke 21:2–4), a prostitute by her shameful lifestyle (Luke 7:36–50), a bleeding woman by her embarrassing secret (Luke 8:43–48), a military leader by his prominence (Matt 8:5–10), a crippled woman by her disability (Luke 13:10–13), or a tax collector by his indiscretions or insecurities (Luke 19:1–10). And he didn't determine his disciples' identity by their previous occupations or lack of education. Jesus taught us that identity is a deeper and more important issue. When their cultural images were shattered, God used their redeemed identity as a powerful testimony in his plan.

This is his desire for all people. He takes those who are "insignificant and despised in the world," and through Christ he rescues them to glorify his name (1 Cor 1:26–31). This is what he longs to do in the lives of teenagers, to deliver them from their social and self-imposed identities and to use them for his honor. And we have the opportunity to participate in his plan for them! But, in order to do this, we must align our view of teens with Scripture and not culture.

Classifying Students' Biblical Identity

While we have considered our culture's confusion regarding the identity of teenagers, the Bible provides some insights to a biblical identity that are both informative and instructive. It's not surprising that the Scriptures give a different picture of human identity than does our society in its classification of students. Therefore, we must carefully consider the biblical perspective and allow it to determine our philosophy of ministry to students and to establish the definition of their identity.

Students Are Spiritually Responsible before God

The Bible does not include the same life-stage classifications that have become the defining standards within our culture. Society typically considers teenagers adolescents, a stage that is inherently ambiguous and stems more from a cultural phenomenon than a biblical paradigm.[1] Scripture does not contain a category that is defined by such a narrow age range. Neither does it accept or excuse irresponsible behavior as a natural part of human growth and development. Instead the Bible teaches that spiritual responsibility before God is expected and should be embraced during this season of change.

The primary biblical passage that most clearly references this stage of life is 1 John 2:12–14. The apostle refers to this phase as young adulthood and distinguishes it from early childhood and seasoned adulthood. John is addressing those of various maturity levels within the body of Christ. While he is primarily referring to their spiritual development, he uses the physical stages of life as a natural

---

[1] For a more detailed consideration of the cultural concept of adolescence, see David Alan Black, *The Myth of Adolescence* (Yorba Linda, CA: Davidson, 1998).

parallel. In so doing, he provides us with a biblical understanding of maturation and classification.

The terms John uses in this passage for "little children" describe them as innocent and inexperienced, in need of nurturing instruction and loving correction. He describes "fathers" as those who are developed in their understanding of God in a way that corresponds to their informed experience in life. But the way he addresses the "young men" in these verses is particularly helpful in defining their stage of life. Young people are categorized as those who have the adult expectations of spiritual responsibility while still developing in their spiritual maturity. They "have conquered the evil one" (v. 13), and they possess spiritual strength along with the ability to comprehend and obey God's word (v. 14).

Other passages affirm a teenager's responsibility before God as well. Similar to John, the author of Hebrews describes spiritual maturity according to physical development. He challenges believers to progress beyond the elementary truths of the faith, milk intended for children, in order to digest the more advanced teachings of Scripture, "solid food . . . for the mature" (Heb 5:12–6:1; cf. 1 Cor 3:1–3). Likewise, Paul affirmed the various stages of adulthood rather than childhood by challenging "older men" and "older women" to disciple "young men" and "young women" within the church (Titus 2:2–8). He also spoke of a more distinct transition from childhood to adulthood in reference to beliefs and behaviors (1 Cor 13:12).

Perhaps the greatest testament to a young person's accountability before God is Jesus himself. As the ultimate model for life and maturity, Jesus exhibited spiritual responsibility at the age of twelve as he sat among the religious teachers, demonstrated understanding, and yielded to his heavenly Father, while still remaining in subjection to his earthly parents (Luke 2:46–51). In doing so, his spiritual development coincided with his physical development as he "increased in wisdom and stature, and in favor with God and with people" (Luke 2:52).

All of these biblical passages equate the spiritual capacity of young people to a spiritual responsibility before God. This distinguishes them from children who are entirely dependent, both physically and spiritually, on others. Teenagers are young people who are spiritually accountable before God, liable for their actions, and capable of spiritual growth and maturity. While this does not classify them as seasoned adults who can shoulder life's responsibilities on their own, it clearly considers teens more as emerging adults than older children. = MINISTRY TO RISING ADULTS

Therefore, we must approach youth ministry with biblical goals and expectations, according to its classification of teenagers. This forces us to evaluate our responsibilities as leaders and our philosophy of ministry. We must focus more on shaping hearts than managing hormones. We must devote ourselves to training and discipling students rather than reinforcing childish tendencies and extending a prolonged stage of immaturity. We must labor and strive to this end, "teaching everyone with all wisdom, so that we may present everyone mature in Christ" (Col 1:28–29).

Students Have Unlimited Potential for God

Not only does the Bible view teenagers as emerging adults who are spiritually responsible before God, but Scripture describes them as those who are able to be used by God in a mighty way. Students are often treated as though they are the "church of tomorrow," as if somehow God's plan doesn't really begin for them until they've graduated from high school. But Scripture recounts numerous examples of how God works in and through teenagers during their developmental years. In fact, the Bible seems to indicate that their potential to be used by God is more unlimited than it is restricted by their age.

Throughout Scripture the capability of young people seems unfathomable by today's standards. For example, at age seventeen Joseph exhibited respectability and reliability in serving his father and his family (Gen 37:2). When given the opportunity for more responsibility, he replied, "I'm ready" (Gen 37:13). After being betrayed by his brothers and sold into slavery, he continued to exhibit these same qualities. In the midst of his hardship and misfortune, "the LORD was with him" and "made everything he did successful" (Gen 39:3). Joseph demonstrated the integrity and faithfulness to God as he resisted extreme pressure and overcame temptation (Gen 39:7–12). As a result, Joseph became a target and suffered undeserved imprisonment, yet through years of suffering, he grew in his faith and obedience. God used Joseph to protect and provide for the people of his generation, but he also used Joseph to facilitate his redemptive plan for Israel. The Lord used Joseph as a teenager, but he also prepared Joseph during those formative years to overcome future obstacles and ultimately to accomplish God's plan for his life.

Daniel provides another noteworthy example. As a young teenager, he and his friends were deported from their homeland and held captive in a pagan culture that attempted to impose its sinful identity on young people (Dan 1:1–7). But, even as a young person, Daniel was mindful of maintaining his faith and devotion to the Lord. He "determined that he would not defile himself" and God granted him favor (Dan 1:8–9). God used Daniel's testimony to influence his oppressors as well as his peers (Dan 1:9–16). As a result, the Lord granted these "young men" wisdom and understanding as he broadened their platform for kingdom impact (Dan 1:17–21). God's faithfulness to accomplish great things through Daniel's life of faith and obedience was largely the by-product of the work he did in Daniel's life as a teenager!

Other examples abound throughout the pages of Scripture. By most estimates when David was a young teenager, he had already demonstrated a pattern of faith and domestic responsibility (1 Sam 17:34–37). He showed courage and spiritual maturity as a "youth" when he fought Goliath (1 Sam 17:33). His faithfulness at a young age propelled him to greatness as a servant of the Lord.

Likewise, as a "young woman" (Esth 2:7), Esther demonstrated faith, responsibility, and remarkable character as a teenager. God granted her favor among the people, she was appointed as queen (Esth 2:15–18), and the Lord used her to deliver the Jews (Esth 4:14; 8:5–17).

Samuel served as a boy in the temple (1 Sam 2:18), came to know the Lord and listened to his voice (3:7–14), and matured and "grew up in the presence of the LORD" (1 Sam 2:21; cf. 3:19). Ultimately he reflected on his spiritual leadership in Israel from his "youth" (1 Sam 12:2). While these examples may have involved exceptional circumstances, they were not exceptions when it came to demonstrating a young person's ability to be used by God.

Similar patterns are evident in the New Testament as well. As we have mentioned, a young teenage girl participated in God's plan for her life. Mary submitted to God's plan to carry and give birth to Jesus: "'I am the Lord's servant,' said Mary. 'May it be done according to your word'" (Luke 1:38). The majority of Jesus's disciples may have been teenagers since only Jesus and Peter were required to pay the temple tax (Matt 17:24–27). Paul had devoted himself to being trained in God's law and was a devout Jew from his "youth" (Acts 26:4). He challenged Timothy that youthfulness was not an excuse for unrighteous behavior (2 Tim 2:22), nor did it warrant being shunned or ostracized by others (1 Tim 4:12). Instead, he affirmed a young person's unrestricted ability to be used by God through serving as an example to other believers.

By contrast, our culture's undefined categorization of teens and its resulting confusion establishes an intermittent stage of life that often relegates students to the spiritual sidelines. Parents, youth pastors, and other leaders often view this season of life as a "holding pattern," one that requires students to keep "circling" in order to avoid crashing and burning. It's reflected in the preventative mindset that approaches the teenage years with the hopes of simply making it through without the students shipwrecking their lives on drugs and alcohol or derailing their lives with life-altering choices and consequences.

While our students will continue to learn and grow within the social constructs of our culture, we are not bound to conform to its model in our discipleship of them. Based on the biblical precedent of God's desire to use young people, and their capacity to be used, our approach should be more proactive than preventative. If we are faithful to disciple them effectively, then we can leverage their spiritual vibrancy, giftedness, and unconstrained faith for the cause of Christ! We can't be guilty of lowering our expectations or diminishing their enthusiasm by discriminating against them because of their age. Instead we must challenge them to live worthy of their high calling in Christ (Eph 4:1), be exemplary in their character and conduct (1 Tim 4:12), and allow God to accomplish unimaginable feats through his power at work within them (Eph 3:20–21)!

Claiming Students' Biblical Identity

When the Bible speaks of identity, it is referring to more than just an image or persona. Because people have been created in the image of God, we possess a unique nature that defines us as spiritual beings dwelling in a physical body. Scripture weds the spiritual essence of our being with our personal existence. As a result, our individual existence is defined more by a spiritual identity (our soul) than a physical one (our body). This is not only an important truth to affirm; it is also essential for our students to understand as they discover and claim their true identity. In 2 Corinthians 5:17 the apostle Paul provides a paradigm for us that can help our teens understand who they are in Christ and the resulting implications. He declares, "Therefore, if anyone is in Christ, he is a new creation; the old has passed away, and see, the new has come!"

The Necessary Element of Their Christian Identity

The opening phrase of 2 Corinthians 5:17 reveals the universal truth of Paul's statement, "Therefore, if *anyone* is in Christ." He separates all people into one of two categories, those who are "in Christ" and those who are not. While being "in Christ" is a possibility for "anyone," the conditional nature of the phrase "if" necessarily implies that it is not a reality for everyone. In the preceding verse Paul had explained that his view of people is solely determined through a spiritual lens. "From now on, then, we do not know anyone from a worldly perspective" (v. 16; cf. 1 Cor 2:2). In other words, he did not define a person's identity by external factors but by eternal factors. "Therefore," he concludes, the essence of someone's identity is entirely based on the existence or the absence of a relationship with Christ.

This means teenagers' identity is not determined by who they are but by *whose* they are! To be "in Christ" is a theological picture of being in a saving relationship with Jesus. It is a positional description that speaks of our union with Christ and engulfs every aspect of our being. It adopts us into God's family, immerses us into his body, and establishes us as his people who are heirs of his eternal kingdom (Gal 3:26–29). Believers are God's treasured possession (1 Pet 2:9) and his beloved children (1 John 3:1). This is the essence of what it means to be a Christian.

Many people, including our students, define the Christian faith in behavioral terms (being good instead of bad) or "destinational" terms (heaven instead of hell). But the Bible defines salvation in relational terms (John 1:12; Gal 4:9), knowing God through his Son (John 17:3). Knowing God is relational. It is not like knowing simple facts about God. It is knowing God through relationship with him. *Therefore, our students must understand that being a Christian is not determined by their best efforts, good behavior, church attendance, or parents' faith. Their Christian identity is established through a saving relationship with Jesus, received by grace through personal faith in his substitutionary death on the cross (Eph 2:8).*

By contrast, the Bible also characterizes those who don't know Christ in relational terms. They are "alienated and hostile" toward God (Col 1:21), "by nature children under wrath" (Eph 2:3), and "enemies of the cross of Christ" (Phil 3:18). As a result of original sin, all people are born with enmity toward God and need to be reconciled through the cross of Christ (Col 1:20). *Therefore, all people, believers and unbelievers, are defined by the nature of their relationship with God and, more specifically, Jesus Christ.*[2]

Many of our students also need us to clarify the difference between knowing about Jesus and actually knowing him. Similar to fans who know their favorite athlete's statistics, career highlights, and personal information, students can learn facts about Jesus's life, the miracles he performed, and the truth that he died on the cross for them. But this does not mean they have a relationship with Jesus

---

[2] Understanding our personal identity in relational terms also corresponds with our unique nature as human beings, created in the image of God, to dwell in personal fellowship with him.

any more than adoring fans actually know their favorite player. Yet, through faith, they can come to know Jesus in a real and personal way. This relationship is the necessary element required to be "in Christ" and defines their personal identity as a Christian.

The New Essence of Their Christian Identity

The next phrase in 2 Corinthians 5:17, "he is a new creation," describes the nature and extent of how a relationship with Christ determines our identity. We must teach our students that salvation is not merely a spiritual decision; it is a spiritual *conversion*. Who we are prior to coming to Christ (characterized by our sinful nature) has been transformed into something entirely different. We are no longer who we once were, and we are now something we previously were not. Jesus spoke of this life-altering change as being "born again" (John 3:3; cf. 1:13). Peter used this same terminology to reference our salvation (1 Pet 1:3, 23). Paul described it as "regeneration" (Titus 3:5), "newness of life" (Rom 6:4), and the "new self" (Eph 4:24; Col 3:10). Our conversion is a spiritual metamorphosis that redefines everything about us (Gal 6:15).

Like an infomercial displaying before and after pictures, the Bible describes the radical transformation that takes place when we come to Christ. Perhaps the most comprehensive picture is seen in Ephesians where our previous identity is characterized as "dead" in our sins, sons of disobedience, and children of wrath (Eph 2:1–3). But, as a result of God's loving mercy, we are made "alive," united with Christ in his glory, objects of God's grace and kindness, and created as a masterpiece in Christ (Eph 2:4–10). Similarly, in Colossians, our previous identity was alienated from God and displayed itself through our sinful actions. But in Christ we have been reconciled and are now considered "holy, faultless, and blameless before him" (Col 1:21–22). And in Paul's letter to Titus, our former lives are defined by disobedience, sinful desires, and hostility toward others. However, in Christ, we are now regenerated, justified before God, and coheirs with his Son (Titus 3:3–7).

Although our students are often aware that a transformed life in Christ has new expectations, we rarely teach them that it also has this *new essence*. Students who follow Jesus have been transformed and are now God's "righteousness" (2 Cor 5:21), his "workmanship" (Eph 2:10), his "children" (1 John 3:1), and "more than conquerors" (Rom 8:37)! As believers, they are not defined by their circumstances, abilities, personalities, or their past. Their identity is not determined by the sins they commit (Rom 7:17), and they do not have to fear any condemnation (Rom 8:1). In Christ they have access to all the treasures of wisdom and knowledge (Col 2:3), they have received every spiritual blessing in the heavenly places (Eph 1:3), and they have dwelling in them the power of God that raised Christ from the dead (Rom 8:11). These are the truths that define our identity in Jesus Christ!

Sometimes our students get the impression that Jesus is in the remodeling business searching for a "fixer-upper." But, when Jesus comes into our lives, he's not simply looking to sand and stain the floors, splash some paint on the walls, and decorate the outside to give our lives some nice curb appeal (see Luke 11:24–26). Jesus is a master carpenter who builds from the ground up. He does not simply renovate your old house; he *relocates* you into a *new* house, giving you an identity that is not the same. He exchanges the run-down, falling-apart shambles of your former nature for a fully furnished, state-of-the-art, glorified mansion that's been bought and paid for with his blood! You may live in the same neighborhood with the same neighbors and streets, but you are completely different.

Sadly the realities of students' new essence in Christ is often overlooked and exchanged for the image they impose on themselves, the reputation others inflict on them, or a perception that their emotions impress on them. But they do not have to be held hostage by these social shackles or phantom personas anymore. They can celebrate as they claim their identity in Christ as a forgiven, loved, valued, and privileged child of the King!

The Natural Effect of Their Christian Identity

The necessary element and new essence of a student's identity in Christ is profound, but it is also practical. Second Corinthians 5:17 concludes with the implications of our new identity in Christ: "The old has passed away, and see, the new has come!" While the verse speaks to the necessary element and new essence in the Christian life, it describes the natural effects of salvation.

Scripture consistently teaches that our new nature in Christ should manifest itself in our behavior. Our former identity has been jettisoned, and its corresponding way of life should likewise be abandoned. "The old" is referring to those actions, attitudes, and sinful affections that reflected our previous nature as an enemy of God. Conversely, our new life in Christ has been established, and we must now adopt a lifestyle that resembles our new nature. "The new" that has come includes those actions, attitudes, and godly affections that accompany our new identity as a child of God, a conqueror, and the righteousness of Christ.

Still, many students struggle with the inconsistency between their identity and their desires. They are convinced that their attempts to live for Christ are really efforts to conceal their sinful nature. But, in fact, the opposite is true! If their faith is genuine, then their remaining struggles with sin are actually the disguise that masks their real identity. The Bible speaks to this spiritual dissonance and the sanctifying process as eliminating "the old self" and embracing "the new self." Scripture instructs us to "take off" the former way of life that was "corrupted by deceitful desires." In turn, we are to "put on" a lifestyle consistent with our new identity, "one created according to God's likeness in righteousness and purity of the truth" (Eph 4:22–24; cf. Col 3:3–10).

This clothing metaphor can be helpful in explaining this concept to our students. For example, after performing outdoor chores on a hot day or exhausting yourself in an intense physical workout, nothing would feel better than to peel off your soiled, smelly, sweat-saturated clothes and take a cool, refreshing shower. After a soapy lather and a clean rinse, no one would ever dry off and then put on those same cold, damp, and grimy clothes. Yet, as believers, many students who have been cleansed by Christ continue to clothe themselves with the filthiness of sin. They wear a foul mouth, a disrespectful attitude, dishonesty, laziness, arrogance, or pride. Too often they clothe themselves with an improper relationship or pollute their hearts with impure movies, music, or other forms of media. But these are those putrid clothes that correspond to their old nature. Instead they should be clothing themselves with Christ's righteousness without making any provision for the sinful desires of the flesh (Rom 13:14).

As fellow believers who are accountable to God, we should teach our students the practical implications of their identity in Christ. Rather than being conformed to the desires of their former ignorance, they are intended to be holy in all their conduct according to their identity in him (1 Pet 1:14–16; cf. Rom 12:2). They are no longer expected to live for their sinful passions but to abstain from them and follow God's will (1 Pet 4:2–4). Because they have been transformed by God's grace, they should "deny godlessness" and "live in a sensible, righteous, and godly way" (Titus 2:11–12). "But as those who are alive from the dead," they are not controlled by sin, and they possess the freedom to overcome it in their lives (Rom 6:11–14).

As a result, our students do not have to perform for God to earn his favor. They can rest in the work that Christ performed on their behalf as they live for him (2 Cor 5:15). They can live boldly for Jesus by simply being faithful to who they are in him! Being authentic, or 'true to yourself,' now means living a righteous life that accurately reflects their true identity in Christ.

Conclusion

When students are introduced to how God views and values them, it liberates them from the cultural teenage stereotypes and frees them to become who the Lord has created and saved them to be. Claiming their identity in Christ and shattering the image they have been living for enables them to fulfill God's will. Since God sees them as spiritually responsible and capable disciples, accomplishing his plan is no longer relegated to a future endeavor; it can be embraced as a present reality. Although students cannot foresee the full extent of his intention for their lives, there are three immediate aspects of God's will that they can begin to pursue.

First, *God's will is for teens to be the best son/daughter they can be*. The Lord's desire for every teen begins in the home. He is fully aware of every student's family situation and desires that their faithfulness to him would begin with devotion to their parents. The Bible commands us to honor our parents (Eph 6:2; Ex 20:12), even if they act dishonorably (Gen 9:20–27), and to obey our parents "in the Lord" (Eph 6:1; Col 3:20). Their spiritual responsibility doesn't alleviate their submission to their parents; it accentuates it. While some students may want to object based on hypothetical or extreme

31

scenarios, a young person's assent to and respect for their parents will condition them to honor and obey the Lord.

In addition, *God's will is for teens to be the best siblings they can be.* God's plan for a student's life also extends into other familial relationships. This not only includes siblings in their homes, but also brothers and sisters in Christ (Rom 12:10). So much of the biblical instruction for believers speaks of the mutual care and compassion we share as a family of faith. Our love for one another is a distinguishing mark as Christ's disciples (John 13:35). Our words to one another are meant to be encouraging and edifying (Eph 4:29). We are to consider others as more important than ourselves by looking out for their interests before our own (Phil 2:2–3). We are challenged to spur one another on toward love and good works (Heb 10:24–25). All of these instructions directly translate into God's desire for our students. As they learn to love their natural and spiritual families, they will learn to be faithful members of God's church and begin fulfilling his plan for their lives.

Finally, *God's will is for teens to be the best students they can be.* Many students feel limited in their ability to achieve God's will because their social life and schedule are dictated by school. But the disciplines of academics, regardless of the subject matter, and the engagement of their school culture are avenues of growth and development that God has accounted for in his plan for their lives. We must teach our students that their circumstances, down to the classmates they sit beside, the teachers they have, and the assignments that are required, have spiritual value that can be redeemed for God's glory (1 Cor 10:31).

The effort and excellence of their work is to be done as unto the Lord (Col 3:23), and they must develop a grateful heart that gives thanks in all circumstances (1 Thess 5:18; Col 3:17). The dedication their schoolwork requires can help them develop the discipline that is vital for the Christian life (1 Tim 4:7–8). Their faithfulness to fulfill their educational assignments demonstrates their reliability and positions them to be entrusted with greater opportunities for the Lord (Matt 25:21). In addition, their interaction with other students allows them the opportunity to share and show the love of Jesus and, thereby, fulfill the great commandment (Matt 22:37–40) and the Great Commission (Matt 28:18–20).

Students' understanding of their identity has enormous spiritual and practical implications for their lives. Therefore, we must help teens expose the counterfeit images they are prone to buy into so they can claim their true identity in Christ and leverage their limitless potential for his kingdom.

CHAPTER 3

Students' Identity in Our Churches

In the early 1990s, missional strategists identified a critical part of the global population that had little to no exposure to the gospel. The geographical area was termed the "10/40 window," a region based on its latitudinal parameters that ranged from ten to forty degrees north of the equator in Asia, Europe, and Africa. The countries and inhabitants of this window were spiritually hungry, many of them suffered under governmental oppression, and many were financially destitute as well. This region became the primary strategic focal point for international missions based on the extreme conditions and the massive number of people who occupied this area.

In recent years missiologists have identified another unreached people group. But it is not a geographical window; it is a generational window. The "10/30 window" refers to an unreached people group who fall in the age range between ten and thirty years old worldwide. Over half of the world's population, 53 percent, is under the age of thirty, and 70 percent of those people are between the ages of ten and thirty.[1] This global demographic is a massive mission field that we as the church have the responsibility to engage. This 10/30 window now constitutes the largest unreached people group in the world, outnumbering the top 100 geographical unreached people groups *combined*.[2]

The sheer volume of unreached teenagers should burden us to pray for the Lord to raise up and send out workers to these fields that are ready for harvest (Matt 9:37–38). As a result, ministering to youth is not a "convenient" option, it is an *urgent obligation*. Pastors and church leaders cannot and should not dismiss or minimize student ministry as a spiritualized social group, extracurricular entertainment option, hormone diffuser, or teenage nursery. Sadly we have heard such descriptions! In our churches we must embrace student ministry for what it is: a spiritual battlefield that requires strategic enlistment and engagement in order to reach and teach young people effectively. But, while we may agree on the enormous need among young people, the church as a whole struggles to find consensus on how we should approach ministry to teenagers. Therefore, it is crucial for us to consider the biblical principles that establish the precedent of student ministry, define its scriptural purpose, and determine its functional pattern.

The Precedent for Student Ministry in the Church

A student's biblical identity as an emerging adult and growing disciple naturally raises the question about the proper place of student ministry in the church. If students are spiritually responsible before God as we discussed in the last chapter, we must ask whether

---

[1] Eric Larsen, *Reaching the 10/30 Window: The Next Generation*, accessed October 31, 2017, mtw.org.

[2] Larsen.

we should even have youth ministry. Hopefully our answer would not be a too quick or immediate "yes!" simply based on either our passion for teens or for job security. Neither of those are sufficient reasons or motivations. Thankfully, we can rely on a scriptural precedent for justifying our ministry to students.

The scriptural identification of "young people" (1 John 2:12–14) that we examined in the previous chapter is enough to warrant their specific consideration within the church. Their category is not explicitly identified in the Bible as a distinct ministry (i.e., youth ministry), but Scripture does endorse demographic-specific ministry with contextual consideration of younger men and women. In 1 Timothy 5 Paul specifically addresses the relationships between all believers and distinguishes them as members of the church family. He encourages older men and women to be regarded as fathers and mothers, while "younger men" and "younger women" are to be treated as "brothers" and "sisters" (vv. 1–2). The mutual relationship shared between these younger believers is to be characterized by godliness and offers horizontal social and spiritual support.

The biblical description of the church family also highlights an important role youth ministry can provide, particularly in a contemporary context. While we will explore the complementary role of student ministry to families more fully in chapter 5, it is important to note its significance here within the church as a family of faith. In a day and age where the nuclear family has commonly deteriorated or fails to provide the spiritual support God desires, student ministry can make a particular and relevant impact on students. Many young people essentially qualify as spiritual orphans and should be ministered to as family members of the local church (Jas 1:27; cf. Isa 1:17). Paul's reference to them as "brothers" and "sisters" affirms their worth as a vital part of the congregation. When combined with a lack of traditional family structure, the church's familial opportunity and responsibility to students is magnified even more.

Paul's instructions to Timothy describes other familial responsibilities of the church as he addresses its particular ministry to "widows" (5:3–16). Although the ministry to those who have lost their husbands is not associated with students or young adults per se, the fact that there was a list (5:9) indicates that churches were encouraged to identify and minister to those who had particular needs that related to particular life circumstances. Paul's later reference to struggles that characterize the young adult stage of life, "youthful passions," implies the elevated need for a particular ministry focused on their needs (2 Tim 2:22). In addition, Paul's admonition to "flee" these desires and to pursue the virtues of "righteousness, faith, love, and peace" further confirms a young person's spiritual capacity and responsibility before the Lord. Therefore, students' genuine potential for Christian growth and usefulness to the Lord, their membership within God's family, and their demographic-specific needs establish student ministry as a biblically valid model.

The Purpose of Student Ministry in the Church

The scriptural endorsement of youth ministry does not automatically authorize all of its contemporary forms or practices. In fact, in order to qualify according to the biblical standards, student ministry must be evaluated based on God's expectations of the church as a whole. In other words, his guiding mandates for the local church must also serve as the benchmarks by which our student ministries are defined.

The church exists as God's covenant people who, by his grace, have individually placed their faith in Christ's atoning work on the cross for salvation and adoption into God's family (Titus 2:11–14).

As God's people we are commanded and compelled to love him and live for him (Matt 22:27–40; 2 Cor 5:14–15). Our primary purpose as Christ's followers is to preach the gospel (Mark 16:15) and to make disciples of all nations (Matt 28:18–20). We devote ourselves to proclaiming Christ and teaching his followers with the goal of helping everyone mature in Christ (Col 1:28–29).

These truths must dictate the purpose of our student ministries. The biblical view of students as capable and responsible believers requires us to approach their discipleship in the same manner as older 'adult' members of the church. This means that the functions of our student ministry must parallel the functions of the church as a whole. When the church was birthed through Peter's sermon at Pentecost and 3,000 people were saved, God's people began to operate according to timeless principles that continue to serve as the functions of the church. Worship, discipleship, fellowship, service, and evangelism should be the active operations that govern all of our ministry practices (Acts 2:42–47).

At the same time we cannot loosely define them with their most familiar descriptions. For example, worship is a lifestyle more than a corporate gathering and encounter (Rom 12:1). Discipleship is more than just a Bible study and should include life-on-life scriptural mentoring (1 Thess 2:8; 2 Tim 2:2). Fellowship must be intentionally spiritual rather than simply being together (1 John 1:3,7), while service should include ministry to both members and nonmembers of our church (Gal 6:10). Similarly, evangelism is primarily accomplished through the ongoing witness of our people rather than limiting it merely to a program (Col 4:3–6).

When properly defined, these five functions can provide a measuring stick for our student ministries. As we evaluate our calendars, every event or activity should accomplish at least one of these purposes. This will enable us to tailor our schedules effectively to achieve spiritual goals while also helping us eliminate those activities that do not actually accomplish the mission. Because of our limited amount of time with students, we must leverage every event as an opportunity for spiritual influence and growth.

Understanding the purpose of student ministry within the church can also help us cast this vision for our students, parents, and leaders. Students will always be more engaged when they have an understanding of the bigger picture. Helping them see their involvement in God's kingdom enterprise will eliminate the small view of student ministry that often limits their ability to make an impact. Establishing an identity for your youth ministry and tagging it with a slogan that captures the Great Commission and great commandment can also help communicate the biblical vision for your group. Members of the church, particularly those who are part of your adult leadership team, can help carry that vision forward as they embrace it as well.

Our mission for youth ministry should reflect the church's mission as a whole since the students are an integral part of the church body. Our vision for the student ministry can also be tailored for teens to provide a sense of ministry identity within the church. This also creates a sense of ownership and buy-in that can be invaluable when helping students envision the magnitude of God's plan for their lives. In addition to embodying the great commandment and Great Commission, a vision statement can also include parallels with the five functions of the church. For example, one of our former youth groups was referred to as GRACE Student Ministry. Students and leaders adopted and embraced the desire to:

Glorify God with our lives, by

Reaching the lost for Christ,

Assisting those in need,

Challenging one another in the Word, and

Encouraging one another in the Spirit.

As you articulate the vision for your student ministry, express the biblical truths with relevant terms in a memorable way. Challenge your leaders to pray for the ministry through this lens and then equip your students to accomplish the mission!

The Pattern of Student Ministry in the Church

Recognizing teens as young disciples and affirming them as full-fledged members of the church raises some important issues regarding our design and philosophy of student ministry. When we overemphasize their demographic-specific nature, we can end up segregating the youth from the rest of the body. Sadly in many churches corporate worship may be the only time students actually engage with other members of the congregation. Even then their interaction is limited as they often sit in the "youth section." In some instances students even have their own worship service tailored for them, and their churchwide interaction is almost nonexistent. If our student ministries are isolated from the body, we will reinforce our culture's mind-set of individualism and entitlement. We will also fail to provide the communal context the family of faith is intended to be. As a result, we will produce self-oriented young people who evaluate a church based on how it caters to their preferences, wants, and desires.

Clearly this is a misguided approach but one that is all too common. Our student ministries should not be *isolated* from the rest of the church; they must be *integrated* with the rest of the church! But offering a demographic-specific ministry that also promotes concurrent involvement can be difficult to envision and even more challenging to implement. There are a variety of factors to consider, beginning with training them to embrace their spiritual responsibility and teaching them how to grow. *The goal of our youth ministry should be to make student disciples of Christ by equipping them to: develop their walk, find their purpose, fulfill their calling, transform their world, and enjoy their journey.* This is best accomplished by facilitating mentoring relationships that conform to the biblical model described in the second chapter of Titus.

The relationships Paul prescribes in Titus 2 are both generational and gender specific. Generationally speaking, the older men and women have a specific responsibility to teach the younger members. The relationships are also intended to train believers according to characteristics and behavior that are specifically related to their gender and God-given roles for men and women. In coordinating these types of relationships, we must create opportunities for intergenerational interaction. We must also identify and equip members of the congregation who will invest in the lives of our students. These mentoring relationships may occur within the context of our existing ministry paradigms through small-group leaders, sponsors, parents, and hosts. We can also enable our youth to develop these relationships by providing opportunities for them to serve the older generation, partner with them in ministry, and learn from them through multigenerational worship and discipleship.

Much of the failure of the contemporary local church to produce a harvest of spiritual fruit finds its root in the failure of its members to understand and fulfill these biblical relationships. The confusion of the biblical roles, the rejection of authority, and the moral collapse in the lives of young people sprout from the malnourished relationships that are mandatory for the health and development of believers in the local congregation.

Even more dangerous is the fact that the problem is a perpetual one. Immature Christians produce immature Christians, and consequently the development of strong and influential believers becomes rare, leaving generation after generation spiritually orphaned. The remedy to this degenerative disease that continues to cripple the church is the healthy and biblical relationships prescribed by God within the church. Older, mature believers must invest themselves in mentoring relationships with the younger believers who, in turn, subject themselves to the tutelage of the older saints (1 Tim 2:2). We must help our students recognize the value of seasoned godliness that previous generations have to offer when they learn with a teachable spirit.

At the same time we must also contextualize our approach for teenagers. We must provide a youthful atmosphere that is inviting to students and their friends that helps facilitate fellowship among them. We should plan events that allow for group participation and welcome guests to an environment that is not intimidating to the unchurched but that nurtures spiritual and relational growth. We must provide activities that will encourage unity, develop relationships, and attract students, which will ultimately lead to spiritual discipleship and maturity. Our teaching, while thoroughly biblical, must work to highlight the relevance of the Scriptures for the unique and specific needs teens face. Integrating our student ministries within the church requires our older adult influences to be balanced and blended with these younger adult realities.

Another factor involved in an integrated approach to student ministry is identifying areas of service and ministry that are suitable for students. When we relegate students to an isolated form of youth ministry, we teach them that they are incapable of being used by God until they are older. However, this violates the scriptural precedent and fails to consider accurately their present value. Encouraging them to sing in the choir, serve as greeters and ushers, minister in the nursery, or contribute in other capacities enables them to grow and mature as capable members of the church now!

In addition to identifying the areas where students can serve, we must also determine what ages or grades should be included in the youth group. This fundamental consideration varies from church to church. And while there is not a biblical standard for age inclusion, some principles can be helpful in determining whether to start your student ministry at sixth or seventh grade.

Not all students are the same age in certain grades, which makes the determination difficult. In addition, there is a broad spectrum of maturity levels within these transitional grades, especially between boys and girls, that further compounds the issue. The complexity of the decision is even greater when you consider the enormous differences between a sixth grader and a high school senior, from their biological development to the challenges they face. These factors cause many parents to feel uneasy about their sixth graders joining the youth group, and, therefore, many churches leave them with the children's ministry.

But, while these obstacles require a delicate balance, they are not impossible to overcome. In fact, it may be necessary when you consider the alternative. Sixth graders' involvement with a children's ministry that is geared for younger elementary grades can mislead them to conclude that the church is childish or irrelevant. Furthermore, these students are typically surrounded by secular middle schoolers throughout the week with minimal reference for what a godly teenager can look like. The influence from their worldly classmates at school will ultimately become something that filters down to the younger children in the church. Therefore, it may be best to include them, being sensitive to their level of maturity but teaching them how they should progress spiritually as they develop physically. It's better to expose them gradually to teenage issues in a controlled and spiritual context with a biblical perspective than for them to be introduced to them in an unrestrained and immoral culture. Plus, the influence of older teenage Christians at church can counterbalance some of the influence they receive at school by providing godly examples that the younger teens can aspire to emulate.

Ultimately the decision will require pastoral input and should also consider the children's ministry. Some churches provide a "bridge" ministry for fifth- and sixth-graders that is intended to help them transition into student ministry. Whatever your church determines is best for your student ministry, it should be a decision that is clearly established and is applied consistently for all members.

The biblical pattern for student ministry requires us to adopt an integrated approach where students are actively discipled through their involvement in the broader ministry of the church. Cultivating a discipleship paradigm requires intentionality and structure, but it should also grow organically as we model mentoring relationships and multiply them according to the scriptural pattern. We must also create and maintain an environment that is designed to meet students where they are and engage them through a contextualized approach. As we do, our student discipleship programs can begin to operate as both a demographic-specific ministry and one that facilitates their growth as functioning members of the church.

Conclusion

Student ministry provides an important avenue to serve and mentor teens as they grow into the young disciples God desires them to be. The biblical precedent of a demographic-specific ministry validates the existence of youth ministry and affirms its potential to be used by the Lord. Integrating students into the life of the church while providing a specialized ministry that addresses their unique needs and learning styles is essential for a student's spiritual development. But, in order to effectively design a youth ministry that accomplishes

God's mission and vision for the church and produces healthy young disciples, we must establish a "target student."

The concept of a target student is not an attempt to identify the types of students we want to reach, but one that defines the kind of students we want to produce. In other words, if you diagrammed the character attributes, personal life skills, and spiritual maturity you desire to see in students that graduate from your student ministry, what would they look like? We all could identify noble traits of the ideal, but we rarely, if ever, consider what is necessary to produce a student that embodies them. Sometimes students graduate from our ministry and we are amazed that they turned out the way they did. While God's profound work in the life of a teenager should always produce awe in our hearts, a healthy young disciple should not be an anomaly that is randomly produced by God's prevailing grace through our ministries. Our "target student" should be exceptional, but they shouldn't be the exception!

The biblical qualities of a healthy disciple are identifiable and can be cultivated by implementing intentional strategies and establishing an environment conducive to their development. If we know the attributes that should characterize a growing disciple who can maintain their personal walk with Christ and fulfill God's will for their lives, then we should design our ministries in a way that focuses on developing these specific traits. This strategic approach should occur on a macro and a micro level. Broadly speaking, our annual calendars and six-year plans that span a student's involvement in our ministry should include a variety of efforts tailored to accomplish specific objectives within their development. This could include grade-specific goals that are designed according to their life situation (i.e., college prep and apologetics for seniors), or it could be devised as a groupwide rotation that cycles every six years.

On a more specific level, all of our ministry programs, from ongoing efforts like small groups and worship encounters to specialized trips and events, should be designed and evaluated based on the particular areas of growth they are intended to promote. Based on their effectiveness, they should be adjusted or abandoned accordingly. Working through this process with a leadership team of parents and sponsors will help them capture the student ministry vision. It will also provide sound rationale for our calendars and budgets as we develop them in consultation with the appropriate leaders. Ultimately, we must let our spiritual goal of producing young disciples determine the ministerial philosophy and practical approach we adopt and implement.

In consideration of this mission and purpose, reflect on this question and pose it to your leaders: How does what we are doing right now help us develop the target student we are desiring to produce? Then proceed accordingly with an unwavering conviction!

PART II.

DESIGNING A STUDENT MINISTRY

CHAPTER 4

Relating to Students

A young man sat in the minivan as his mom and older brother walked into the church office to meet the new youth pastor. As the young minister introduced himself and began to inquire about the family, the mom confessed that the younger brother was hesitant to meet him. Initially the youth pastor assumed that he was shy or easily intimidated, but in a moment of transparency the mom disclosed the real reason. She explained that the middle schooler was skeptical and refused to come in, defiantly speculating, "Why should I get to know him? I'd probably like him, and then he'll leave like everybody else!"

Over the next several years the student pastor would spend time in the student's home playing video games, giving him rides to church events, and investing in his personal growth and maturity. The Lord used their years together to help the student develop as a young man, and their relationship became one of formative influence that transcended his teenage years. The impact of the student was equally influential on the youth leader as he learned to appreciate the incalculable value of personal relationships in ministry forged through sacrificial investment over an extended time.

This young student's initial apprehension is not uncommon, and it is not unfounded either. Too many student pastors and youth leaders unintentionally, but oftentimes irresponsibly, establish rapport with students only to tear away prematurely from their post and emotionally wound the students who had come to trust and revere them. While some of the relational hurt of ministerial departure can be unavoidable, the real disappointment often stems from the failure of youth leaders to recognize the sacred trust, critical significance, and foundational platform for all ministry relationships.

The personal bond that is formed with students will largely determine the effectiveness and success of a youth pastor's ministry. But relationships with students are often volatile and fragile. Therefore, relationships must be pursued and preserved with the greatest vigilance. This requires us to understand the biblical foundation of relationships, their ministerial purpose, how to establish them, and how to leverage them for Christ and his kingdom.

Created for Spiritual Community

We are created in God's image (Gen 1:26–27). While this unique characteristic includes moral, intellectual, and governing capacities, the *imago Dei* is primarily a relational capacity. All people are designed to dwell in personal fellowship with God, and this distinguishes us from the rest of creation. Our personal faith in Christ's atoning sacrifice on the cross is necessary to be reconciled to God (Col 1:19–20). As we continue to walk by faith, we can abide in fellowship with God through love and devotion to Christ (John 14:23).

As God's people, we also share another relational distinction. Through the indwelling presence of his Spirit, we are joined together with one another and exist as one body (Eph 4:4–5). Communal fellowship with other believers reflects this spiritual reality and is an essential part of our spiritual growth. Therefore, we must faithfully gather together as God's people, exhorting and encouraging one another to grow in our faith (Heb 10:24–25). Ultimately, our personal fellowship with Christ will result in our communal fellowship with one another (1 John 1:7).

Our relational nature as people, along with our spiritual fellowship as God's people, is the necessary basis for dwelling as an authentic community of faith. These same truths must serve as the basis for forming community in our student ministries as well. Therefore, our goal in establishing relationships with students is primarily to help them recognize their created purpose of dwelling in personal fellowship with God and the essential role of communal fellowship with his people for their spiritual growth and development. Within an authentic community of transparency, students will be moved from a profession of faith to a passionate pursuit fueled by faith in Christ.

The life of a believer was never designed to find discipleship outside the community of faith. The idea of someone possessing and maintaining personal independence is foreign to the idea of biblical discipleship. In many student ministries and churches, the sharing of life is relegated to being in a small group, discipleship class, or Sunday school. But being in a community of discipleship involves much more than attending a gathering. The twelve disciples lived within the dynamic of close proximity for the purpose of intimacy and accountability. This transparency and authenticity within community created a dynamic that is missing in many of our churches and, more specifically, our student ministries today. Therefore, it is vitally important to teach our students that every disciple is called to share life with other believers; and we, as leaders, must work to provide a context that allows them to experience true community.

Challenges for a Student Community

While we are created for community, this does not mean authentic community occurs automatically. As a result of our sinful nature, along with cultural conditioning of autonomy and antiauthoritarian mind-sets, living in fellowship with others becomes extremely complicated. In student ministry this is compounded even more by its unique nature, which inherently involves both normative and sinful threats to unity. In order to establish a ministry environment that facilitates genuine spiritual community among students, it is necessary to identify these threats and determine how to neutralize them.

Ministry to teenagers is fundamentally difficult because of a combination of intrinsic factors that are spiritually benign. For example, the disparity of ages, various levels of maturity, and a broad range of differing personalities are common disparities that make establishing community among students a daunting challenge. Youth ministry must also consider other normative factors that make students individually unique and collectively diverse, such as gender, ethnicity, and socioeconomic status. Added dynamics associated with multiple school districts and communal rivalries require our consideration as well. While none of these are prohibitive factors to living in spiritual community together, they do present some natural barriers to students' dwelling in harmony.

In addition to the normative challenges, a variety of sinful factors can threaten the unity of a youth group. Scripture teaches us that relational issues, quarrels, and disagreements primarily result from the selfish and sinful desires within us (Jas 4:1–2). The Bible highlights the intense and controlling nature of these fleshly desires among young people, so it shouldn't surprise us that our teens continually engage in divisive arguments and senseless debates (2 Tim 2:22–23). Teenage social drama and relational dysfunction can be characteristic of their age, but they also reflect their natural disposition toward selfish and sinful behavior. Our culture also reinforces this self-centered mentality. These natural tendencies and social influences typically result in common teenage behaviors like jealousy, gossip, betrayal, and persistent agitation. These are all common toxins that sabotage the unity of any youth group.

Divisions and disagreements can also stem from preferential or prejudicial treatment among God's people (Jas 2:1–9). Systemic and specific forms of discrimination in our culture and our churches can influence our students to judge others with superficial and hypocritical self-righteousness (Matt 7:1–6). As a result, our groups can become poisoned by battles for popularity, exclusive cliques based on social or spiritual criteria, or an elitist mentality that celebrates talent and ability over commitment and humility. When our ministries begin to focus on individuals and their personalities, abilities, or possessions rather than on Christ, divisions are certain to occur (1 Cor 1:10–17). Sadly youth pastors or magnetic leaders can become the idolized objects of students' affection. Many times they are elevated as ministry celebrities who soak up the spotlight and leave the students in the dark while the true Star of the show, Jesus, is relegated to a supporting role (at best!) in our self-glamorized productions.

All of these lethal threats to unity, particularly in youth ministry, are even more perilous given the lack of spiritual and emotional maturity students typically possess during their formative stage of life. And when you combine these community toxins with the normative threats to the unity of a youth group, authentic community in student ministry seems next to impossible to achieve. But recognizing these threats allows us to effectively consider how God intends for us to neutralize them as we make "every effort to keep the unity of the Spirit through the bond of peace" (Eph 4:3).

Cultivating a Scriptural Community

In order to overcome these threats and achieve unity, we must first recognize that true unity cannot be created by our effort alone. No matter how many interpersonal skills and leadership gifts someone may possess, no one can manage or manipulate people, much less teenagers, to foster genuine community. This is because biblical unity is a spiritual unity, one that is formed and established on a spiritual basis instead of superficial factors. A common faith in Christ, joint submission to his lordship and leadership, and authentic fellowship in his Spirit are defining characteristics of true community. These spiritual essentials establish the context for genuine relationships to form and develop with our students.

But this means that while authentic community cannot be created by our effort alone, it can be cultivated. Paul challenged the Philippians to adopt a common spiritual mind-set, join together in collaborative gospel efforts, and pursue the sole purpose of fulfilling their mission in order to live in authentic community (Phil 1:27). Likewise, we must promote this mentality with our students by modeling it in our own lives and mentoring them to embrace it for theirs.

A single-minded focus on the gospel will strengthen our personal relationships with them as we mutually seek to deepen our personal relationship with Christ by fulfilling his mission. This ultimately will enable us to enjoy the spiritual oneness that Jesus prayed for us to experience, that we may be "completely one" as we exhibit the love of Jesus for one another as a testimony to the lost world around us (John 17:21–23).

We must also challenge our students collectively by emphasizing missional opportunities for our groups instead of fellowship opportunities. For example, we should consider dedicating summer trips to those of the missional variety rather than simply providing "camp experiences." If we challenge our students to live missional lives but do not provide them with opportunities to grow in sharing their faith, then we are only challenging them with shallow lip service to the Great Commission. As a result, their unity will be equally thin.

In addition to a common missional focus, authentic community is also fostered through a mutual submission to God's Word. Imagine an entire island of people that absolutely, wholeheartedly treasures the Word of God. The Bible is more than a just book of truth to them. It serves as the life source of all things to the point of simulation, application, and preservation of doctrine. The ultimate goal of this entire civilization is to be a people group that lives in the victory Christ proclaimed. They consider the entire Word of God and the principles within as the foundation of every decision. They allow the Scriptures to shape their lifestyles, their choices, their entertainment, their workplaces, schools, hobbies, and relationships.

Now, take this group of people from this island and transport them to America, introducing them to several churches and congregations. Allow these two cultures to collide and see if there are any similarities or any points of contention. In most of our faith communities there would most likely be a major disconnect from the perspective of a society that sought to live by the principles of the Bible versus a society dangerously familiar with the Bible.

Therefore, our efforts in attempting to do relational ministry within the structure of student ministry must change. We cannot simply attempt to promote unity through a shared experience centered on entertainment and emotion. We must help our students adopt a submissive disposition to God's Word that enables them to grow in understanding and obedience. As they do, our teens will draw closer to one another through a shared perspective, but they will also experience a deeper spiritual unity as their hearts resonate with one another over the truth of Scripture. By promoting a common devotion to God's mission and his Word, we can help cultivate a biblical community for students that he desires and intends.

Commissioning Our Student Community

As we are joined together by our corporate faith in a common Savior, we become a mobilized army to fulfill Jesus's clearly articulated mission (Matt 28:18–20). What is commonly referred to as the Great Commission is more than a methodical plan. It's an ordained strategy to change the world one person at a time! The model established by Jesus was to move his followers to a course of action found in his command to "make disciples." This must become the heartbeat of our student ministries and the goal of our influence and investment. In other words, we are to "make disciples" of students who will then "make disciples" of others.

The apostles of the early church believed this command of Jesus was indeed serious. They devoted themselves to teaching God's word and training disciples without compromise (Acts 2:42; 6:4). The practical game plan for discipleship was also embodied by Paul and explained in his instructions to Timothy. "What you have heard from me in the presence of many witnesses, commit to faithful men who will be able to teach others also" (2 Tim 2:2). Timothy was to replicate Paul's investment in him by discipling others who would in turn faithfully disciple others.

This single and simplified goal helps our students understand the objective of the global campaign strategy set forward by Jesus. It is more than making converts, adding adherents to a religion, or recruiting participants in our ministries. Our ultimate purpose is training passionate followers of Jesus Christ. In order for us to effectively make disciples, we must adopt our Lord's threefold strategy: "go . . . baptize . . . teach."

As you are *going*, actually describes the ongoing efforts of every believer to join in Jesus's mission through an evangelistic lifestyle that faithfully shares the gospel without hesitation or discrimination. *Baptizing* admonishes all believers not only to follow Christ in believer's baptism, signifying and symbolizing their conversion experience, but also to challenge believers to identify with Christ publicly as they are immersed and assimilated into his community of faith. *Teaching* involves more than the dissemination of information. It is intended to be a life-on-life discipleship that informs and instructs young believers with biblical truth that trains and transforms Christ's followers.

This strategy and mission for making disciples is gained and gleaned through personal investment modeled outside a youth group meeting in a church facility. Discipleship is sharing life with the intention of passing on values, beliefs, character, and integrity while passionately pursuing Jesus. As the familiar maxim states, discipleship is indeed more "caught than taught." Therefore, in order to shape student believers as they mature in their faith, it is essential that we adopt the biblical model of investment and instruction through personal relationships. While we are limited in the number of students we may be able to mentor personally, we must enlist other leaders who will invest in our youth with this same mentality and approach.

But what does personal discipleship involve? It requires a person investing a great deal of time, energy, prayer, and commitment into the life of another person. It includes more than just sharing the gospel with others. It requires developing a relationship where the student being discipled learns, grows, and draws closer to God (1 Thess 2:8). In this model the person discipling sets the example, and the student learns and grows. This type of discipleship follows the biblical model for spiritual investment, transformation, and replication. As Paul reminded the Thessalonians, "For you yourselves know how you should imitate us: We were not idle among you; . . . instead, we labored and toiled, working night and day . . . to make ourselves an example to you so that you would imitate us" (2 Thess 3:7–9).

In this model of discipleship, we mentor students and invest everything we know and have into them while encouraging them to do the same thing in the life of someone else. This is perhaps the greatest advantage of the personal discipleship model: the ability to mentor and shape another person and then send him or her out to do the same for someone else.

Being actively involved in the lives of the young people God has called you to disciple requires that you do so by walking in close proximity. Nothing can ever substitute for the ministry of presence. Therefore, understand that relevance is not Starbucks, trendy haircuts, smoke machines, or laser shows in worship services. Instead, it is meeting students at their core need that will require us to selflessly give our time, energy, and efforts for their sake. It most certainly will involve our attendance at their sporting events, hanging out at their places of interest, and sharing personal conversations in appropriate settings. But it will also extend into the messiness of their lives as we walk alongside them when they suffer through loss, heartache, failures, and disappointment. These experiences will strengthen our relationship with them and foster personal trust that we should help them translate into a deeper faith in Christ.

Missional living and personal mentorship always requires sacrifice. As we willingly offer ourselves to our students, we also perfectly communicate the sacrifice epitomized in the gospel. Jesus was the greatest missionary and contextualizer in history. He became flesh and dwelt among us (John 1:14), spoke our language, and sacrificially gave his life to give eternal life to all who call upon his name (Phil 2:5–11). This must be our adopted model of involvement for the sake of investment that allows us to connect with teens and make disciples who will in turn make disciples.

Conclusion

Building relationships with students is important for a variety of reasons. Personal relationships are a significant aspect of their social maturation as we encourage their holistic development. Relationships also help cement their commitment to the church and their involvement in the ministry based on the meaningful friendships they establish.

Perhaps more importantly for us, relationships become the ultimate platform for our leadership and ministry. Jesus demonstrated how personal relationships can be leveraged for the goal of making disciples through personal investment. Jesus saturated his mission in love, kindness, mercy, and grace toward others. He demonstrated compassion for them because he recognized the desperate nature of their condition and their need for sacrificial love and spiritual leadership (Matt 9:36). Jesus was moved to meet their physical needs that not only reflected a deeper spiritual need but that would also provide an avenue for personal investment into their lives.

In the same way, our ministry must mirror his heart and approach. We should serve God while serving students by meeting their physical and social needs with a keen eye toward meeting their ultimate spiritual need. This must become the underlying philosophy that dictates our relational approach to student ministry. It is within garnered trust that we are able to implant biblical truth modeled within the stresses of cultural collisions of conformity. This allows God's truth to be received not just as information transferred but as revelation through relationship. Students will listen to our teaching more readily when they have a personal relationship with us. They will share their struggles and trust our counsel when we have a relationship with them. They will also embrace our vision and follow our leadership more readily when our relationship with them is authentic.

Therefore, we must devote ourselves to developing personal re-lationships with as many students as possible. We should invest in our most devoted students, faithfully reach out to and engage sporadic attenders, and welcome first-time guests with a relational and hospitable spirit. For some students our relationships will be more organic and will become deeply meaningful and personal. For others our relationship may remain more cordial and familiar. But we should be approachable and accessible to every student, looking for points of contact and common interest, demonstrating a personal interest, and displaying a willingness to invest in them.

CHAPTER 5

Reaching Families

T he youth pastor listened as the young middle schooler fought back tears to share his prayer request in a small group of peers he barely knew. The student was heartbroken for his dad who had gone out the previous night drinking with his friends. He wanted to see God change his dad's heart, but he didn't know what to do. He hoped his new friends at a church his mom had started bringing him to could help. The group listened, and the youth pastor melted for the young man and his situation.

Over the next several years the young man would become a faithful member of the group. His mom began to serve when she could as a sponsor and volunteer, and his younger brother even got plugged-in. Collectively the youth pastor and the family began a conspiracy of love to reach their dad. They invited him to events, but he was uninterested. The leader attempted to befriend him when he dropped his boys off from time to time, but he remained distant. Eventually he began to soften toward the group and accepted the invitation to be a grill man at a weekend event, and he met a few other dads and parents. More than six years later the young youth pastor, who had transitioned in ministry to a different church several states away, received a voice mail asking him to call the recently graduated former student. As he returned the call, the young man's voice trembled in a similar fashion to his initial prayer request years earlier. But this time he expressed the joy and relief of the life-changing news, "My dad got saved!" Years later the former youth pastor and entire family would rejoice together at the grace of God and the work of his hand through their faithful prayers and persistence.

You do not have to serve in student ministry long before you realize that youth ministry is about something far bigger than teaching teenagers. It is about reaching families. While this young man was instrumental in his dad's coming to faith in Christ, sometimes it works in reverse. Still other scenarios involve ministering to students who come from broken homes, blended families, or contentious situations that are resistant to the faith. But *every* student represents a family unit of some kind that is intended to be a foundational part of the student's spiritual journey and formation. Therefore, we have the obligation to leverage our ministry with the students to support, strengthen, and/or supplement their natural families in order to fulfill God's intended design for their spiritual growth and development.

But it's not uncommon for the relationship between parents and youth leaders to seem strained. Sometimes student pastors can feel as though the parents' expectations for them are unreasonable and unrealistic or that parents aren't supportive of their efforts. Parents can struggle with student leaders whom they perceive to be overstepping their relational boundaries or undermining their parental efforts. The sad reality is that lost in the tension between parents and youth pastors are the students who lose the complementary benefits that mutual support and cooperation can provide. Therefore, in order to safeguard our ministries against unnecessary friction, we must adopt a mind-set that doesn't detach the student from the parents but recognizes their inseparable nature as we minister to them both.

This will best be accomplished when we recognize the primary role of the family in the spiritual development of their children, empower them to achieve this purpose, and supplement their efforts by uniting the complementary functions of the church with those of the family.

Shared Functions for the Church and Family

The five functions of the church we identified in chapter 3 as essential aspects of our mission and vision for student ministry are also critical facets of spiritual development within the family. These five functions—evangelism, discipleship, fellowship, service, and worship—are intended to be cultivated within the family as the primary context for spiritual formation in the life of a student. As a result, these shared functions can serve as the bridges for cooperation between the student ministry and a student's family. In our effort to minister to families, these areas serve as inroads for influence.

The Evangelism Bridge
The primary function exhibited by the early church was evangelism. The apostle Peter, empowered by the Holy Spirit, preached to the masses at Pentecost with great fervency, urging them to repent and be saved (Acts 2:38). A great outpouring of God was displayed, and the masses were saved and baptized to identify in the saving work of God. The early church was moved with a sense of urgency to share the greatest news ever, and through their faithful testimony God continued to add to their number daily those who were being saved (Acts 2:47). But note that the offer and assurance of salvation was promised "for you and for your children," confirming God's desire to reach the lost through the family (v. 39).

God's design has always been to perpetuate the faith through the family (Deut 6:4–9, 20–25). Therefore, today's family unit must embrace the perspective that evangelism within the home should be parents' highest priority. The thought-provoking challenge every Christian parent faces is the reality that there is no guarantee their child will forever walk in obedience to the Lord Jesus Christ. One may draw some comfort from Proverbs 22:6, "Start a youth out on his way; even when he grows old he will not depart from it." However, this verse is a guiding principle, not a guaranteed promise. Just because we bring our children up in Christian homes does not automatically mean they will become Christians or godly adults.

Salvation is the work of the Lord, and apart from the work of the Holy Spirit in the life of that child, there is no salvation. The role of Christian parents is first to decide for themselves that they will serve the Lord and dedicate their home to creating an atmosphere of Christ-centered activity. This provides the child every opportunity to trust Christ for salvation by creating an atmosphere that exudes the lordship of Jesus through the daily routines and rigors of life. Parents must also extend and encourage a decision for personal faith in Christ while being careful not to coerce or convince their child to take a premature or pressured step of faith.

Likewise it is important for a student pastor to prioritize evangelism as a primary goal. Leading young people to know Jesus not just intellectually but personally must be woven into every aspect of our ministry. Inviting students to trust Christ is accomplished through personal appeal but also by putting Christ on display and seeking to draw students in with a message of hope in Jesus. By teaching how the gospel can transform the daily rhythms of life from mundane to meaningful allows the family context ultimately to become missional. As a result, our evangelistic efforts will cooperate with and complement the parents' attempts to reach their students with the gospel.

The early church was founded on this principle of evangelism, seeking to leverage relationships for the opportunity to share Jesus. While the bond between youth leaders and students will be strong, it cannot compare with the parental platform. Therefore, as the gospel is preached within the student ministry context, we must encourage our parents to adopt the same sentiment and shared vision within the home, making the most of every opportunity to share the good news of Jesus with their children (Col 4:3–6).

Sadly, our efforts to reach families and their students are often impeded by misguided attempts to be more compelling. Due to a concern of being offensive or pushy, the church has camouflaged the gospel in seeker-sensitive terminology, thereby unintentionally emasculating the power of the cross. Youth groups have adopted gimmicks and become cheap imitations of a culture that values experience and entertainment over substance and significance. But we must always remember: *what we win them with is what we win them to!* We cannot compromise the truth and the mission for the sake of attraction and attendance. When we model this type of approach, we consequently cause our families to fall into a mind-set that they have to do the same thing. As a result, parents lose confidence in the power of the gospel and become less intentional about modeling and sharing the message of Christ in their lives and in their homes.

God is not looking for slick presentations or for Jesus to be made cool. He is looking for a church that is comprised of families that desire to make him famous. In an effort to do so, a churchwide emphasis must be placed on the principles of *invest and invite*. This is the effort of every member to notice people that God strategically places into their life for the purpose of sharing the good news of Jesus. When parents live this way before their children, then evangelism is more caught that taught. Students will witness the power of the gospel through their parents' testimonies and daily example of sharing their faith with others. Likewise, parents will be inspired by the efforts of their youth to be faithful witnesses for Christ in their schools and among their peers. This evangelistic zeal will perpetuate itself within the church through the complementary efforts of the student ministry and the families of youth. Most importantly, it will result in authentic life change and spiritual transformation.

The Discipleship Bridge

The second function of the early church that serves as the blueprint for every student ministry and every family raising teenagers is discipleship. Evangelism finds its fulfillment in the process of discipleship. Discipleship is often regarded merely as a Bible study, accountability group, or training course. While these can be integral parts of a discipleship emphasis, these examples are platforms for understanding and developing the true essence of biblical discipleship—learning to follow Jesus in faithful obedience. Programs and organized small groups can be effective, but discipleship is most formative when there is a shared experience outside of the organized attempt of formal investment.

This is why family discipleship is so essential for a teenager's spiritual growth. Life-on-life discipleship occurs more organically through the daily interactions and shared experiences of a family. And no one is more qualified to be the principal agent of spiritual investment than the parent. God designed the home to be the primary context through which faith would be nurtured and perpetuated. He endowed parents with the responsibility of teaching their children the truth and training their children to walk in it (Deut 6:4–9). Furthermore, God's Word instructs parents to raise their children in the discipline and instruction of the Lord (Eph 6:4).

Since a teenager's parents bear the primary responsibility for their student's discipleship, a youth pastor's primary role must then be seen as one that equips and encourages parents in their efforts of spiritual formation. Though student ministries may attempt to simulate opportunities and discuss them in reflective or theoretical conversations, they can never be replicated to the degree that they naturally occur in everyday life within the home.

While clearly the home is intended to be the primary context for spiritual formation, this does not negate the vital role a student ministry can play in a teen's discipleship. Student pastors and youth leaders must also serve as spiritual mentors who not only faithfully share the gospel but who also fully invest themselves in the lives of those they serve (1 Thess 2:8). In order to shape teenagers to become mature in their faith, student ministry leaders need to invest a lot of time in them. This is not intended to supplant the family but to supplement the family. The role of youth leaders is a complementary one that should actively build relationships with students that can be leveraged for Christ in partnership with parents. Through the combined efforts of parents and church leaders, students will have every opportunity to grow in their faith through the tutelage of both their natural and their spiritual families.

Therefore, discipleship in student ministry is training students to trust and obey the principles of God's Word through a personal relationship with Jesus Christ. This is essentially a shared purpose with the home of the student. As youth leaders, we have the responsibility to develop a strategy that implements the discipleship purpose of the early church contextually within our own ministry. We then can invite parents to partner together in an effort to disciple their students at home as we provide additional avenues for spiritual growth within the church.

Discipleship is sharing life with the intention of passing on values, beliefs, character, and godly behavior through a passionate pursuit of Jesus that facilitates Christian maturity. When the student ministry and parents are co-laboring in this same direction, there is a high probability that students will remain attached to the local church after high school. Instead, students will be equipped to grow deeper in their spiritual commitment to Christ and will model the investment made in them by discipling others (2 Tim 2:2).

The Fellowship Bridge

The third function of the New Testament church in the twenty-first century is the commonly misunderstood concept of fellowship. Many churches assume fellowship is an inevitable by-product of the other four functions—evangelism, discipleship, service, and worship. However, the modern understanding of fellowship is not what the early church practiced or intended. First-century believers approached fellowship with a spiritual understanding and an intentional mind-set that produced genuine community, or *koinonia*, the way the Lord intended.

The early church "devoted themselves" to the fellowship with the same dedication as their commitment to "the apostles' teaching" (Acts 2:42, 46). In other words, fellowship did not just happen the way many churches today expect it to occur whenever believers are together in the same room or at a common event. Most student ministries just presume fellowship to be a ministry strength because they provide well-attended activities. But, for instance, what distinguishes a secular Super Bowl party and a church Super Bowl party that qualifies as fellowship cannot simply be the choice of beverages or a half-time Bible study. Therefore, in order for our youth groups, families, and the contemporary church at large, to regain its influence and impact, we must adopt a redefinition of *fellowship*.

The spiritual reality of our common salvation in Christ unites us together as a family of faith (Eph 4:1–6). This unity in the Spirit that believers share is the basis for true fellowship (Phil 2:1; 1 Cor 13:13). In addition, our personal fellowship with Christ and our continued pursuit of deeper intimacy with him draw us into interpersonal fellowship with one another (1 John 1:6–7). So, as we individually walk with Christ and devote ourselves more fully to him, we join together with other believers on the same journey and experience a spiritual connection that edifies and encourages us. From a practical standpoint this means that when we gather together, true fellowship occurs when we are intentional about provoking one another toward love and good works as we seek to build one another up in our faith (Heb 10:24–25). Otherwise, despite the enjoyment we may get out of being together, it doesn't constitute biblical fellowship!

Since we experience fellowship through our spiritual union in Christ, and this reality constitutes a family of faith, fellowship has a direct parallel to our students' families that we must leverage within our ministries. This is best demonstrated within God's design for the family. Biblical community, reflective in the home, exhibits shared resources, not just in a materialistic sense but one of spiritual, emotional, and physical support and stability (Acts 2:44; 4:32). When students have a home life that does not serve these purposes, our student ministries can provide it for them. For those who do have a healthy, Christian home, our ministry can serve as an extended family that provides additional support and encouragement that fosters spiritual growth.

An effective student ministry that embraces the purpose of the early church with regard to fellowship must seek to create a dynamic where healthy relationships, marked by mutual service and sacrifice, can flourish. A student ministry that seeks to build community by promoting and practicing hospitality is magnifying the purpose the family was intended to accomplish. A family on mission that seeks to share life at the table with one another and seeks to invite others into this dynamic teaches their students to live with an "apron mind-set" instead of a "bib mentality." An "apron mind-set" says, "Let me serve you!" By contrast, a "bib mentality" says, "Serve me!" By catering to students' desires and demands, we must be careful not to promote the selfish "bib mentality" that will sabotage any attempt to promote genuine fellowship.

To change the culture in our student ministries, we must regard fellowship as more than free food and games. Instead our times together must be seen as opportunities to deepen one another's faith by serving the needs of others through humility (Phil 2:3–4). This epitomizes what family is all about! Therefore, we must lead parents to promote a spirit of hospitality in their home by having people over for fellowships and gatherings for the simple purpose of serving others. In doing so, families will begin to reach families, and students will begin to serve in practical ways that create a culture of invitation and intentionality in our student ministries.

The Service Bridge
The fourth purpose of the early church that serves as a bridge into reaching and serving families is ministry. As God's New Testament covenant community was established, they were meeting one another's needs and serving those around them (Acts 2:45). They were willing to extend themselves to extreme levels of personal sacrifice and expense for the sake of others. Likewise, we are called to shoulder one another's burdens (Gal 6:2) and take advantage of every opportunity to minister to all people, especially those of the household of faith (Gal 6:10). In doing so, we fulfill the law of Christ and publicly display the gospel through tangible acts of kindness.

The example of ministry was best exemplified by King Jesus himself, who was willing to empty himself (Phil 2:7) and come to serve rather than be served (Mark 10:45). He modeled humble and willing service as an example that we might also gird ourselves with the servant's towel to minister to others in his name (John 13:12–17). This mind-set is to be the perspective in which believers are to approach daily life. We are called to "love one another deeply" and to "outdo one another in showing honor" (Rom 12:10). The current culture competes for position, prominence, power, and prestige, while Christ calls believers to die to personal agendas and ambitions in order for his kingdom to advance. A key reason for the exponential growth within the early church was their unified spirit of sacrificial love in the body of Christ, which was characterized by their servant's heart toward one another. We must train our students to adopt this Christlike disposition through sound biblical teaching, through effective modeling of service in our own leadership, and by providing our students with opportunities to minister to others.

Most parents envision their youth's ministry to others as service opportunities within scheduled events such as community projects or mission trips. These are effective ways of doing ministry, but the purest form of ministry is simply being open and observant to providential opportunities God provides. They do not always take place either on calendars or with passports' being stamped but are most often daily encounters in everyday routines of life. This does not minimize the importance of a student ministry's scheduling opportunities for service locally or abroad. Those activities or trips can often create the awareness and motivation for students to minister in their daily contexts. But ultimately, in order for our student ministries to reflect the ministry principles of the early church, we must seek to instill this ministerial philosophy into our families.

As student pastors, we must challenge our students and their parents to serve others as a family. When they do, families will begin to see that the best way to combat materialism in the heart of their student is through exposure to ministry outside of their familiar context. We should lead our families to look for opportunities to serve by volunteering at a local ministry partner or perhaps even to take a family mission trip in place of the typical scheduled vacation. We must also recognize that efforts of service can become avenues of outreach to engage other families and their students. Through loving acts of kindness that embody Christ, we can open the door to assimilate others into the church body that may not otherwise attend our typical services or events.

If our ministry leads students and their parents to be pushed out of their comfort zone, then families will be transformed through a displacement of what has typically been important no longer being as valuable. When students are challenged to elevate the needs of others, to sacrifice their own wants and desires, and to engage people who live differently and may be less fortunate, God will perform genuine heart change through ministry exposure. Therefore, we must look to partner with our families to emulate the early church by serving others in practical ways. As we do, we can begin to see how the functions funnel together through our collaboration—evangelism leads to discipleship, discipleship creates community, and community should do the work of ministry.

The Worship Bridge
The functions of the early church all culminate in the ultimate goal of bringing glory to God through the final purpose—worship. A life lived for the honor and fame of Jesus is expressed through daily actions of glorifying him (1 Cor 10:31). But the early church also recognized the importance of corporate worship as they encountered

God's presence and power and celebrated his greatness as they gathered together (Acts 2:43, 46–47). It is unfortunate to notice the dissention within the Western church over such trivial issues such as worship style. This would have been foreign to the early church as their gatherings were characterized by joy and unity. But when preference takes precedence, it always leads to dissention and division.

Unfortunately, most "worship wars" are fought between the student ministry and the rest of the church. Students in every generation prefer fresh manners of musical expression, while older adults often have years of familiar preference that condition them as loyalists who can easily become legalists. But style should never trump substance. Paul affirmed a variety of stylistic expressions, "psalms, hymns, and spiritual songs," as long as they were informed and infused by "the word of Christ" and were offered with grateful hearts (Col 3:16).

Since much of the tension regarding worship within the church is often attached to student ministry, we must take the mantle of responsibility to begin to return to biblical worship. This resurgence will be most effective when we are able to help the parents of teens see themselves as integral parts of the process by helping to shape a worship culture in their home. We must equip parents to understand that what we do privately should fuel how we respond publicly. And what parents model for their children with regard to worship, either in the pew or in the home, will determine how their students approach God in their daily personal walk or their weekly corporate worship.

The context for the first use of the term *worship* in the Bible is both informative and instructive regarding this issue. Abraham was called to sacrifice his only son, Isaac, on Mount Moriah. When he arrived, he spoke to his servants, saying, "The boy and I will go over there to worship" (Gen 22:5). Note that while Abraham took the wood, the fire, and the knife, there were no instruments. The praise of worship from God's perspective was that a willing servant was willing to honor God by obeying his voice. There at Mount Moriah, Isaac, with many questions, submits himself in faith. He places his full trust in his earthly father who is fully trusting his heavenly Father. Oh, that our student ministries would get this concept. Isaac responded in worship, obedience, and sacrifice because it was first modeled by his father!

As student pastors and leaders, we must come alongside our parents in modeling worship as life and life as worship. That which we exhibit in everyday practice will be emulated by our students in their personal obedience and corporate worship. Then we will lead a generation who is shaped by a culture of worship that is founded on substance not style. And as we invite parents into this understanding, our student ministries and churches will experience a spiritual harmony achieved by obedience through sacrifice that blends more beautifully than any particular genre of music ever could.

Conclusion

The five functions we have explored in this chapter are the birthmarks of the early church, and they must be hallmarks of our student ministries. While every ministry may have particular functions that they excel at more naturally, our goal must be to become well rounded and holistic so that the body of Christ is not dysfunctional or disproportionate. But the ability of the church to serve in these capacities will depend on the individual members of the church reflecting the same holistic approach in their own spiritual walk. Evangelism, discipleship, fellowship, ministry, and worship should all be areas where every believer seeks to grow personally so that the church can then grow corporately. When the lives of individuals are spiritually lopsided, the church will suffer from the same spiritual imbalances.

For students, individual maturity in each of these areas will best be accomplished when the church family and the domestic family are mutually committed to fulfilling their role in training teenagers to be faithful followers of Christ. Student ministries can help facilitate this cooperation through the common responsibilities they share with parents as summarized in the five functions of the church. When we leverage these essential functions as bridges into families, our partnership with parents will become advantageous instead of adversarial. Our joint efforts to disciple students will be exponentially more effective through consistent reinforcement and a spiritual network of support. In addition, God will expand our ministries beyond the teenagers we disciple to include the families of students we have the privilege to serve. May we be found faithful!

CHAPTER 6

Recruiting Leaders

L ike any other ministry in the church, student ministry will require, and in many ways depend on, servants of Christ who selflessly volunteer their time, energy, and resources. Sadly many youth leaders, especially those who are younger, do not appreciate the sacrifice required for people who have full-time jobs, busy family lives, and other obligations that deserve their attention. Some student leaders are grateful for the investment others are willing to make, but deep in their prideful hearts, they believe they can lead the group on their own with minimal help from others. They view themselves like (and sometimes behave like!) the youth ministry superhero who can carry all of the weight and never grow weary. Both of these perspectives often have the same result: exhausted and frustrated leaders, neglected or absentee students, and disrespected or underappreciated parents and volunteers.

God does not intend for his church, or any ministry of it, to operate this way. God designed his church to rely on all of its members who function as invaluable and integral parts for the building up of his body (Eph 4:11–16). As student ministry leaders, we must recognize that the growth and impact of our ministries will largely

depend on our ability to raise up, recruit, and rely on others to partner with us in our efforts to reach and teach students.

Depending on Leaders

Depending on others is not an indication of weakness; it is a sign
of strength. If our student ministries are going to grow, we must
recognize that we will not physically be able to maintain healthy
relationships with every student. We must also be willing to admit
that not every student will be able to relate to us (or even like us!).
But the more diversity we have in our volunteers, the more likely it
is that every student will have someone with whom they can relate
and trust.

A significant resource of student ministries across the land is
an untapped reservoir of available leaders from whom we can draw.
This reservoir of leaders shares a vested interest in the success of the
ministry in terms of teenage lives changed by and for Jesus. Who
am I speaking about? I am talking about the resource of *parents!*
Parents serve as the primary pool of volunteers who can provide the
help we need to build a healthy youth ministry. Since our student
ministries should primarily be viewed as extensions of the home,
it is only right and responsible to enlist family members to help
disciple teenagers.

Many parents are willing and available to help but have never
been asked. Other parents hesitate to get involved because they do
not want to overstep perceived boundaries with their students. Some
are intimidated by the thought of working with teens, discussing
sensitive topics, or dealing with the hormonal attitudes that can flare
up at any moment. But a good youth leader will learn how to subtly
disarm their fears, ease their reservations, and find ways to include
them in the ministry.

While parents should not be the only volunteers we involve, they should be the primary sponsors we recruit. Other leaders like young adults, college students, or seasoned church members can offer distinct advantages as well. Sometimes these volunteers may have more flexibility in their schedules, they may relate more easily to teens, or they may provide wisdom from their years of experience. These types of leaders will also be necessary to help establish a strong and sustainable student ministry.

Various kinds of leaders are not only necessary because of the diversity of students and their needs, but different aspects of our ministries require multiple forms of support that individuals may be uniquely qualified to offer. Relational support is the primary area where most youth pastors need help. Those who serve in this capacity should be personable, encouraging, available, and have a genuine love for students. We also need leaders to serve as logistical support. These leaders typically have administrative gifts, exhibit the heart of a servant, demonstrate responsibility and resourcefulness, and potentially provide strategic assistance through a particular skill set. Perhaps most importantly, we need ministry partners who can offer spiritual support. These individuals will be prayer warriors who undergird the ministry and leadership by interceding on our behalf. They will be grounded in Scripture, offer godly counsel, openly share their faith, provide encouragement, and serve as models of spiritual maturity for our students.

These various forms of support, along with the wide array of attributes necessary to minister to a diverse group of student needs and personalities, can make identifying potential leaders a daunting task. This can be even more difficult in smaller communities and churches. Therefore, we must take a strategic approach to identifying leaders to serve in student ministry.

Drafting Leaders

One of the most important skills a student pastor can develop is learning how to recruit leaders effectively. Most youth ministries depend on volunteers who are willing, but may not necessarily be called, to serve in student ministry. Sometimes we inherit leaders who have served in a capacity for years and want to operate based on "how it's always been done." While we never want to exclude those who make themselves available, we do want to consider prayerfully those whom God may be leading to serve with our students and provide them with the opportunity.

The process of identifying these individuals can be involved and requires careful discernment. But the investment on the front end can save us significant time and spare us from headaches in the future. It is a lot harder to ask a volunteer to step back than it is to step up. And it is easier to water areas patiently than it is to put out fires frantically that are sparked by well-intending, but ill-equipped, leaders. Too many times we recruit out of necessity or find the first volunteer who can plug a hole rather than prayerfully identifying those who are gifted and called for specific roles within our ministries. So we should adopt a few simple principles that can help us navigate the recruiting process.

One of the most important principles for enlisting volunteers is that we should always recruit in person. General announcements from the platform or in the bulletin will invite anyone to participate. While we would not exclude people from serving in some capacity, we also must recognize that everyone cannot serve in any capacity (e.g., teaching, see Jas 3:1). So it is best practice to identify qualified individuals based on the nature of our need and to discuss the possibility with them. As we describe the specific opportunity, it is also important to communicate the vision for our student ministry and show them how this particular service will help us achieve our mission. People will be more willing to invest their time and efforts when they can see how they fit within the bigger picture.

A common mistake many people make when recruiting leaders is to undersell the role. In an effort to persuade them, we can be tempted to minimize the time it will consume, the effort it will require, and the difficulty it may entail. But, when we do this, we are also subtly communicating that *anyone* could do it, and we are minimizing the significance of the difference they can make. While we should not exaggerate the importance, we should be honest with people regarding the amount of time that will be necessary, the investment it will require, and the potential impact they can have. We must be considerate of their family commitments and career demands while also giving them time to consider prayerfully the possibility without the pressure to make a spur-of-the-moment decision.

We must also be particularly aware of the parent-student dynamic whenever we are recruiting parents of youth in our group. Parents must consider whether their presence on a trip or in a Bible study will have a stifling impact on their student's willingness to share or restricting effect on their freedom to forge relationships with their peers. They must also understand that while a leader never stops being a parent, sponsors are required to be more than parents. Their attention cannot be focused solely on their student. Their involvement must consider the group as a whole, and they must be willing to serve accordingly. Having this conversation up front can spare you from an awkward conversation after a misunderstanding that could have been avoided.

One final recruiting principle involves dealing with those who approach you about volunteering with the students. It's always a good practice to ask them to contact you later to discuss it further. This gives them the opportunity to demonstrate genuine interest and provides you with evidence of their commitment and follow-through. After you discuss their desire to serve, invite them to participate in a general capacity. Asking them to begin by observing areas of need and engaging students relationally can reveal their motives and prove their willingness to serve. Those who are simply looking for a position of status or are more interested in their agenda than the students will grow impatient and will look for other ministry capacities in which to serve. But those who exhibit a servant's heart and a genuine passion for the students can be affirmed and integrated into the ministry with confidence.

Developing Leaders

The passion that drives most student pastors is a desire to see God transform the hearts and life trajectories of teenagers. Undoubtedly, the most encouraging triumph for a youth pastor is not high attendance at a recent event, a renovated room in the church dedicated to students, or the money donated to the latest fund-raiser. It is the testimony of students whose lives have been radically altered by the good news of Jesus Christ. But, in order to maximize our influence with students, we must also recognize that more students can be changed by the gospel when we are leveraging our leadership to impact those who can in turn multiply the investment into more students than we could ever reach by ourselves. This must be the driving motivation behind our efforts to develop leaders, and it must become the vision they embrace in order to fulfill the mission.

Leadership development within student ministry begins with clearly articulating this biblical vision for teenagers and inviting people to join in the cause. Identifying the "target student" we described in the third chapter establishes the goal we are attempting to achieve. Still, the practical steps of accomplishing the vision require us to organize a strategy that can make it a reality. Determining these steps may be unique to your particular context and situation based on resources, pastoral support, and student demographics. But pouring into leaders who then pour into students is the transferrable principle Jesus established and modeled.

If we recruit volunteers and sponsors who faithfully serve, but who ultimately stand back and watch us disciple the students, then we are creating an unhealthy youth ministry that is vulnerable to collapse. This is because these student ministries are built on the cult of personality—particularly the student minister's personality. But what if the personality goes away? What if God calls a student minister to another church, or there is another situation in which the student minister is gone? There is a vacuum in leadership, and the ministry is vulnerable. Student ministries that are built on a leader's ability and persona are not sustainable models. Such models can create an unhealthy spiritual codependency for the teens who begin to associate growth with a particular individual and often detach from the body of Christ when they graduate.

But contrast the cult of personality with a student ministry vision that raises up multiple leaders. Such a vision provides a model of biblical discipleship within a spiritual community where their walk is ultimately dependent on one individual, and his name is Jesus! That is a model that is biblical and sustainable.

Most parents and youth leaders are intimidated, overwhelmed, or inexperienced when it comes to discipling teens. So, if we cast a vision of mentoring students, then we bear the responsibility of equipping our leaders to achieve the mission. While pouring into our leaders may involve our helping them grow in their faith, most often it will be helping them relate to students, showing them how to communicate effectively, and guiding them through the process of spiritual mentorship. In other words, we may not spend the majority of our time teaching our leaders biblical truths, but we may need to show them how to effectively lead a small-group Bible study. We may not need to counsel adult sponsors on alcohol, drugs, or sexual temptation, but we may need to help them consider how to communicate with teens about these issues in a biblically informed, sensitive, and responsible manner. These are the types of fears and responsibilities that keep adults from volunteering to serve in student ministry. Parents and potential leaders do not have to be culturally savvy, but they should be biblically and practically prepared to accomplish the mission of discipling teenagers.

Once people have bought in fully to this vision, the next step is to help facilitate a sense of ownership by making something conceptual become practical. Invested and involved parents will then become focused on the group goals rather than the individual aspirations they have for their own children. They will also begin to enlist their fellow parents to be a part of what they recognize is bigger than any one family. As youth leaders, we must understand that we need this type of buy-in from our leadership base that will translate into a high level of cooperation, contribution, support, and networking ability. Ultimately, all of these things help us accomplish our mission of transforming the lives of students.

It is also important for us to recognize that this spiritual "game plan" won't run without opposition. Opposition is, after all, a reality in ministry that we all must consider and understand. For example, a young youth minister was about to be hired to serve his first church when the senior pastor told him, "If we called Jesus himself as the youth pastor here tomorrow, there would be people who would be opposed!" Opposition and ministry go hand in hand. It is just part of the deal. There will always be those who consider it their spiritual gift to chastise the student pastor and make his life difficult. But, as we learn to rely on the Lord, exercise wisdom, and communicate regularly with the senior pastor, we can continue to pursue the mission in faith. We must not be distracted by those who would attempt to hijack the mission, and we must discern how best to handle those who are less than cooperative while maintaining our patience and resolve (1 Thess 5:14). God can use every situation, no matter how sticky or ugly, to accomplish his purposes and propel the mission forward.

Redeemed conflict can have a galvanizing effect on a student ministry, and we must see ourselves as God's instruments of peace in achieving a resolution that preserves the mission. Many leaders are offended at a deep level when they face resistance due to insecurities concerning personal leadership and, unfortunately, never learn to respond appropriately to tension in a positive manner. Most ministers avoid the conflict by choosing to run from the situation and relocate their services to another youth ministry. But instead, servant leadership empowers communication to transpire between individuals with deep concerns and gradually seeks to lead them to partnership. Fight or flight are the typical responses to conflict, but we can learn to welcome points of contention for the purpose of developing spiritual fortitude and curating the vision. Spiritual formation in the midst of conflict is a reality we can embrace as part of our responsibility as leaders who develop leaders!

Deploying Leaders

Once the vision is clearly communicated and adopted, it begins to possess inertia and momentum. In order to provide a level of stability and fortitude, the infrastructure becomes essential. As visionary leaders, we must not only be able to communicate the vision, but we must be secure enough to give it away. A partnership that links arms together with others begins with a level of trust and a willingness to delegate responsibility. This requires mutual trust, transparency, and vulnerability that create instant credibility with people seeking to be part of something larger than themselves. They now envision themselves as vital ingredients for success rather than as a means to an end.

One of the most important steps youth pastors can take, especially early on in their ministry, is to establish a leadership team. This team should be small enough to manage, should consist of trustworthy and reliable volunteers, should include a variety of types of leaders, and should possess spiritual depth and perspective. There are enormous benefits to pulling a team like this together. These leaders can hear your vision and help you refine it. They can provide feedback for your ideas and events before you actually implement them. The parents on the team can give you insights and intel from their students, feedback the youth would never share with you otherwise. Many times they will understand your decisions and help insulate you from criticisms as they respond on your behalf when they hear them. And they can help share your vision as they interact with other parents and leaders within the church.

These teams must be prayerfully selected and personally recruited. It may be necessary to sensitively filter the members you include. Consistency is important in building momentum, but sometimes having members of this team participate on a rotating basis may be helpful. When this team is established and operates well, it can be one of a youth pastor's greatest assets in ministry.

In addition to a leadership team, youth pastors must strategically deploy leaders by developing a ministry infrastructure. For most ministries this will not require an elaborate organizational chart. Coordinating how various volunteer positions fit together to accomplish the vision can be extremely helpful for recruiting support and placing sponsors. Even for churches who aren't currently large enough to require this type of organizing strategy, it can be helpful in preparing for and facilitating growth. Strategic volunteers can breathe life into a ministry area and help it develop. Creating positions without people to occupy them also operates in faith and trusts the Lord to raise the right people up to fill the strategic roles.

In order to create an infrastructure, the student pastor may have several coordinators who oversee particular areas of ministry responsibility like activities and events, discipleship, outreach, and service projects. The activities coordinator can help schedule events, organize the calendar, and manage logistics. They may also help line up families to bring snacks or secure sponsors for the events. The discipleship coordinator can assist the youth pastor by evaluating curriculum, recruiting small-group teachers, and planning studies and series. Similarly, the evangelism coordinator can help direct outreach events, manage guest follow-up, organize mission trips, and lead prayer efforts for lost friends and family members. The service projects coordinator may help identify ministry opportunities, schedule workdays, and handle logistics for projects.

This type of model provides support for the youth pastor with coordinator positions who collaborate together as active partners in ministry. These roles also represent areas of oversight that may include other volunteers. Organized leadership structures like this provide sustainable stability to the ministry, empower volunteers to serve according to their giftedness, position the ministry for future growth, and disseminate the burden of leadership. Delegation of leadership also helps leaders avoid ministry burnout, shares ownership of the ministry, and frees the youth pastor to focus on aspects of the ministry that are uniquely his responsibilities.

All of these forms of shared leadership require us to be willing to trust others with the responsibilities we sometimes want to reserve for ourselves. We also have to let go of a perceived celebrity status that can be emotionally intoxicating in order for us to elevate others to places of ministry prominence and influence. Our willingness to empower others demonstrates a Christlike strength in our leadership that refuses to operate out of pride, insecurity, or fear. Our desire and efforts to see others succeed in our ministries will result in a larger number of students being reached and discipled. It will also be a testimony to our students that will encourage them to adopt a similar disposition of confident humility as they learn to serve and minister to others.

Conclusion

Jesus's ministry is famous for his supernatural miracles and life-altering messages. But perhaps the most transformative aspect of his ministry is not seen in his isolated encounters and powerful expressions. His daily investment in his followers that equipped and empowered them to exponentially multiply into others is the leadership paradigm that continues to expand his kingdom two thousand years later. Jesus came to lead by serving others. His humble devotion empowered his disciples to join his mission and become effective leaders of the same kind. He taught his followers that their leadership would be evaluated according to their willingness to serve (Matt 20:25–28). Therefore, as ministry leaders we must recognize that the greatest measure of our leadership will be demonstrated in our service to others and empowering them to fulfill the mission of discipling students.

This investment and multiplication model is the discipleship strategy God intends for us to adopt and implement in our student ministries. In order to do this, we must depend on leaders for support, draft leaders as ministry partners, develop leaders through personal mentoring, and deploy leaders for the work of the ministry.

Particularly in student ministry, the value of raising up leaders cannot be overstated. From collaborative partnerships with parents to forming influential relationships with students, mobilizing leaders will be one of the most significant and strategic aspects of our ministry.

PART III

DISCIPLING IN STUDENT MINISTRY

CHAPTER 7

Teaching Them to Walk

E very parent knows the joy of watching their child take their first steps. The staggering and stumbling as they learn to balance on their own, the ability to pick themselves up when they fall, and the sheer excitement of experiencing their world from an upright position are all priceless moments to cherish. But a toddler's becoming mobile also creates a whole new set of challenges for the parents. The toddler now possesses the ability to go almost anywhere and get into everything! Opening new doors (literally and figuratively!) reveals a world beyond toddlers' imagination while also exposing them to realities they may not be prepared to handle. Taking steps is one thing; taking on stairways is another!

Working with students involves a similar dynamic that requires balance. When we disciple teenagers, we are attempting to help them grow roots and wings simultaneously. Some critical facets of spiritual development among teenagers are: (1) being spiritually grounded in their faith, (2) being personally integrated into our church, and (3) being spiritually discipled in their family.

At the same time, as student ministers, our goal is to move teenagers towards an embraced responsibility for their faith, equipped with the necessary skills and resources to propel them forward as they transition into their next stage of life.

Following high school, many students relocate, which can require them to detach from their church home and adapt to distance from their immediate family. Their success during this season of adjustment and their ability to acclimate in new surroundings will largely depend on how well we have discipled them and taught them to walk. Therefore, we must carefully consider how we might best prepare them to passionately pursue God's will for their lives while maintaining an intimate love for Jesus and devotion to his church.

Our Goal for Spiritual Disciplines

As we consider the characteristics of our "target student" that we want to see graduate from our student ministries, the foundation of every attribute will be their spiritual growth and maturity. But, unlike their physical development, their spiritual growth does not happen involuntarily. Sanctification is an intentional and intense process that requires understanding, training, and perseverance. The essential skills and tools necessary for spiritual growth and development are what we often refer to as *spiritual disciplines*.

The concept of spiritual disciplines more than likely has a negative connotation among our students. This is understandable since *discipline* usually conjures up thoughts of punishment and restrictions. But, when understood from a parent's perspective, discipline is an act of love that is intended to be corrective, formative, and redemptive. This ultimately reflects God's heart for discipline, for "the Lord disciplines the one he loves" (Heb 12:6). While Scripture acknowledges that discipline is not comfortable, it also confirms it as necessary and beneficial: "No discipline seems enjoyable at the time, but painful. Later on, however, it yields the peaceful fruit of righteousness to those who have been trained by it" (Heb 12:11).

These same concepts undergird our understanding of the spiritual disciplines. The pursuit of Christ is often referred to through concepts of training and perseverance. It is compared to that which requires grueling effort and personal discipline like that of a long-distance race or a boxing match (1 Cor 9:24–27). Likewise, we are repeatedly challenged to adopt the mind-set of those who practice self-discipline such as athletes, soldiers, and farmers (2 Tim 2:3–6). But, instead of physical effort that offers some earthly benefit, we are instructed to discipline ourselves spiritually for the eternal purpose of godliness (1 Tim 4:7).

We must be careful to remind our students that their positional status in Christ is already one of holiness and righteousness. Performing spiritual disciplines does not make us godly in this sense. As Christians we are called to align our practical righteousness in life with our positional righteousness in Christ in order to "be holy" (1 Pet 1:13–16). In other words, we must teach them the proper understanding of justification (declared righteous) and sanctification (becoming righteous) so that they understand the nature of spiritual growth and the role of the spiritual disciplines as essential steps in the process.

While godliness is the goal in terms of outcome, we must also teach our students the proper goal of the spiritual disciplines in terms of motive. Many times, in our devotional habits, our motivation can easily become misguided and tend toward legalistic exercises of self-righteousness. Since students are conditioned to evaluate their success based on our performance, this can become an even greater tendency in their lives. We must help them to understand that it's not out of duty or obligation that we follow Christ through the spiritual disciplines, but out of love.

God's love for us is unconditional and was proven in Christ's substitutionary and atoning death for us on the cross (1 John 4:10; Rom 5:8). The practices of personal devotion are a reciprocated response to Christ's love for us (2 Cor 5:14) and our expression of love for him through obedience (1 John 5:3). This is why the ultimate command is for us to love God with every fiber of our being (Matt 22:37–38) because our devotion to him will flow from our love for him (John 14:15). For those whose hearts have been captured by God's love, our mind-set toward the disciplines changes from "I've *got* to do this" and becomes "I *get* to do this." We have been set free from the bondage and burden of sin in order to surrender to him and serve him (Rom 6:6–13). Therefore, spending time with him and serving him becomes a privilege and opportunity we are compelled to do out of love and gratitude with the ultimate goal of becoming more like Jesus!

Our Growth through Spiritual Disciplines

Once our students understand that sanctification is the process of being made holy, conforming to godliness in the likeness of Christ, we must teach them how spiritual transformation actually occurs. It happens just like every other work of God, "'Not by strength, or by might, but by my Spirit,' says the LORD" (Zech 4:6). In our "do it yourself" (DIY) culture that teaches our teenagers that "you can do anything," we are raising up a generation of self-reliant teenagers who don't know how to cope with the reality of their own inability. Some may be more motivated than others not to give up and to keep trying, but ultimately we must teach them that we can't do anything apart from Christ (John 15:5; Phil 4:13) and the power of his Spirit. Romans 8 teaches us that in and of ourselves we are powerless, but we have the Spirit that raised Jesus from the dead living inside of us, empowering us to live for Christ and accomplish his will (Rom 8:1–11).

Tragically, because of the abuse and misunderstanding of the doctrine of the Holy Spirit, many churches (especially youth groups!) avoid the third person of the Trinity altogether! Confusion about the person and work of the Spirit has led to a spiritual phobia (and we don't mean a reverent fear) regarding his role. As a result, most Christians fail to acknowledge the Spirit, much less rely on him. But his work is critical to our spiritual growth. The Spirit indwells us (Rom 8:9; 1 Cor 6:19), he fills us (Eph 5:18), he empowers us (Eph 3:16; Rom 8:11), he leads us (Gal 5:18; John 3:8), he counsels and comforts us (John 14:16, 26), and he produces spiritual fruit in our lives (Gal 5:22–23).

When it comes to the spiritual disciplines, the Spirit is God's power by which we are to practice them and his presence by which we encounter him. His Spirit is how he speaks to our hearts (Rom 8:16). The Spirit is who enables us to pray and he intercedes on our behalf when we don't know how to pray (Rom 8:26–27). Only through his Spirit are we able to understand spiritual truths (1 Cor 2:10–16). God sent the "Spirit of truth" to guide us and give us understanding of the Scriptures (John 16:13). He discloses Jesus to us (John 15:26) and ultimately, by the power of God's Spirit, we are to be conformed to the image of Christ (2 Cor 3:18; Rom 8:29).

The spiritual disciplines are the means through which God's Spirit works to accomplish our spiritual transformation. We must also remember and teach our students to understand that neither the exercises themselves, nor our efforts to perform them, are what transforms us. They are simply the avenues that position us beneath God's transforming grace, which ultimately performs the work of sanctification (Titus 2:11–14). The disciplines have no power in and of themselves, and our disciplines have zero ability to accomplish spiritual transformation. We cooperate with God's grace as active participants through the practice of spiritual disciplines to become who he has made us and saved us to be (1 Cor 15:10; cf. Phil 2:13). Therefore, we must teach our students that God's Spirit and his grace perform the work of sanctification in us!

Our Guidance in Spiritual Disciplines

Every student ministry is looking for the formula for godliness, or the ready-mix version of it, in an effort to lead students to biblical maturity. We must affirm the reality that Jay Adams asserts, "You may have sought and tried to obtain instant godliness. There is no such thing. . . . We want somebody to give us three easy steps to godliness, and we'll take them next Friday and be godly. The trouble is, godliness doesn't come that way."[1] As Jerry Bridges notes, it comes at a cost: "No one becomes godly without commitment to pay the price of the daily spiritual training which God has designed for our growth in godliness."[2] The spiritual disciplines that serve as the avenues for growth are those holy habits we encourage for our students, but many times we fail to provide adequate training to help them know how to practice them effectively. Our ministries must equip students to be faithfully devoted to the foundational spiritual disciplines.

Communing with God in *prayer* is an essential part of every believer's walk. Jesus frequently and faithfully prayed during his earthly ministry (Luke 5:16; Mark 1:35), and he even spent extended time in prayer (Luke 6:12). Through Christ we can approach God's throne with confidence and can appeal to him for our needs

---

[1] Jay E. Adams, *Godliness through Discipline* (Grand Rapids: Baker, 1973), 3.

[2] Jerry Bridges, *The Practice of Godliness* (Colorado Springs: NavPress, 1983), 34.

and requests (Heb 4:14–16). God invites us to pray and assures us that he will answer us as a loving Father (Matt 7:7–11). We can bring our concerns to him and find peace in his presence (Phil 4:6–7; 1 Pet 5:7). God calls us to pray continually (1 Thess 5:17) and promises that our prayers are powerful and effective (Jas 5:16), and he provides us with basic principles for how we should pray (Matt 6:5–13).

As those who are training young disciples, we have a responsibility not only to show our students their need for prayer, but we must also show them how to rely on God through passionate and persistent prayers (Luke 18:1–8). We must explain the various types of prayers (1 Tim 2:1; Eph 6:18) and provide practical tips for how to pray (e.g., adoration, confession, thanksgiving, supplication, praying out loud, prayer journal, etc.). We must not only encourage them to spend time in devotional prayer; we must model it for them by leading them in prayer. We should also show them how to pray corporately as they: *listen* to their fellow believer's prayer, *echo* it in their heart, *add on* as the Lord prompts them, and *personalize* it for themselves in its application (LEAP). Considering the importance of prayer and these practical principles, there may not be a greater service we can provide for them than teaching them how to pray.

We must also teach them how to spend time in *personal Bible study*. Most students don't enjoy reading in general, much less when they perceive the Bible to be an ancient book that is difficult to understand. However, the Bible is God's chosen means for salvation (1 Pet 1:23; 2 Tim 3:15) and for sanctification (John 17:17; 1 Pet 2:2). Students must learn to revere it as God's divine self-disclosure (2 Tim 3:16) that is living and powerful and able to pierce their hearts with convicting and correcting precision (Heb 4:12). We must also teach them to love the Scriptures and to build their lives on them through submission and obedience (Matt 7:24–27; Jas

1:22–25). It is the recipe for success in the Christian life, and there is no substitute for what it provides (Josh 1:8; Jas 1:25).

In order for these things to happen, we must teach our students how to submerge themselves in Scripture. We must show them how to read God's Word daily through a regular Bible reading plan and explain how exposure to the Scriptures will change their lives. They must learn how to read it devotionally with application and reflection resources. Gradually they must also be taught how to read it deeply, to dig into a passage and navigate Scripture through cross-references, word studies, and other theological tools for understanding (2 Tim 2:15). A life that is submerged in Scripture must also be saturated with the Word through memorization and meditation. This will root their lives in the life-giving truth of the Bible, nourish them with truth and understanding, and produce fruit that satisfies their souls (Ps 1:2–3).

As they become saturated in the truth, they must also learn to submit to God's Word. It is reliable and trustworthy as it reveals God's will and guides us through life (Jas 1:22–25). It is also invaluable, and it should be treasured as God's Word as they learn to listen to and obey his voice (Ps 19:7–14). Ultimately, our students will learn to love the Scripture by how we teach our Bible studies, through the passion we exhibit for it, and the role it plays in our lives!

In addition to prayer and Bible intake, we must teach our students the practical obedience and consistent devotion to other fundamental disciplines as well. We must provide them with opportunities for *service*, enabling them to discover and refine their giftedness while ministering to others. Discipleship in the life of a follower of Jesus Christ is a direct call to servanthood. (Matt 20:26–28). Jesus demonstrated this in loving acts of service and commended his disciples to do the same for others (John 13:1–17). Our students must learn how to consider others as more important than themselves and how to look out for the interests of others above their own needs and desires (Phil 2:3–4).

We must also teach them how to *worship* in Spirit and in truth (John 4:23–24). This includes both corporate worship with other believers and personal worship as a daily lifestyle that glorifies God. Our students have to learn that the substance of praise songs is more important than their style (Col 3:16). They must learn how to tune their hearts to worship even if a song is performed out of tune. We must teach them how to worship as living sacrifices, offered on the daily altar in a way that glorifies God and is transformed for his glory (Rom 12:1–2; 1 Cor 10:31). This will only occur when we provide the proper understanding of obedience and faithfulness, consistently teaching them how to honor God in their hearts, with their lives, and with their praise (Heb 13:15).

Another spiritual discipline we often encourage our students to practice, but rarely equip them to do, is *evangelism*. Perhaps the greatest indicator of our students' spiritual maturity, and thereby the greatest testament to our efforts to disciple them, will be their commitment to share their faith. We may rightly emphasize our marching order from King Jesus to "make disciples" (Matt 28:18–20), but we must teach them how not to be ashamed of the gospel (Rom 1:16). Although their godly lifestyle should be a testimony that brings glory to God (Matt 5:16), we should also challenge them to be bold in their witness. We should teach them how to rely on the Spirit (Acts 1:8) by praying for witnessing opportunities and for praying for wisdom toward outsiders (Col 4:2–6). They must be taught how to explain and defend their faith in a respectful way as they engage the lost world around them (1 Pet 3:15–16). The best instruction will ultimately be our examples as we model spiritual conversations, tell our stories, and invite others to trust Christ. Evangelism, along with the other core disciplines, can't simply be spiritual habits we promote; they must be practices we explain and demonstrate.

Conclusion

The foundational disciplines are essential for our students to progress in their personal walk with Christ. Therefore, we must be faithful to encourage and equip them to practice the spiritual devotions. We must also be careful to properly explain the role and the goal of the disciplines so that our students don't slip into a legalistic or self-righteous mentality.

We have the exciting privilege of cultivating a discipleship culture with the understanding that this current generation has been empowered to change the world. When they begin to faithfully position themselves before the Lord and learn how to devote themselves to the spiritual disciplines, they will be transformed into the likeness of Christ and will be used by the Lord to transform the world around them. Then, as spiritual mentors, we will be able to declare, "I have no greater joy than this: to hear that my children are walking in truth" (3 John 4).

CHAPTER 8

Teaching Them to Think

I magine you are planning to take a trip. You pack the car with
everything you'll need to enjoy your time away. You're ready to
go. But what if you plugged the incorrect address into the app on your
phone? You can follow the directions carefully, enjoy the scenery along
the way, but you'll never actually reach your desired destination. All
of your packing and plans won't help you get there. Your desire to be
there won't magically make it happen. You will end up confused and
frustrated because you took all of the prescribed steps believing they
would take you to the place you desired to go. But, if the address is
incorrect, the *right* steps are actually leading you in the *wrong* direction.

Spiritually speaking, this is why theologian A. W. Tozer asserts,
"What comes into our minds when we think about God is the most
important thing about us."[1] Essentially, Tozer is contending that everything else in life flows from our view of God. If our convictions
about God are inaccurate, all of our efforts to live for him will be
in vain. They will unintentionally, but inevitably, be misguided and
will result in our living a life that never actually achieves our desired

---

[1] A.W. Tozer, *Knowledge of the Holy* (San Francisco: Harper Collins, 1961), 1.

goal of glorifying God. But, if our conception of God is accurately based on his revelation through Christ and the Scriptures, then our life can be lived as an offering of acceptable worship that pleases and honors him (Rom 12:1–2).

This is why theology is so critical, especially in the life of a teenager. The trajectory of their lives will largely be determined by what they believe about God. Therefore, we must carefully consider *why* we should teach them theology, *how* we should teach them theology, and *what* we should teach them about theology.

Why Should We Teach Theological Doctrines to Our Students?

All too often youth leaders will focus on teaching topical studies in an effort to guide their students with practical application. But we cannot afford to sacrifice theological truth on the altar of relevance. A pragmatic approach to teaching the Bible often turns into group counseling sessions that discuss social issues and produce deistic moralists. However, sound theological teaching provides the necessary basis for properly understanding God's practical instruction. This approach recognizes that their beliefs will determine their behavior, thereby combining both theological truth and practical relevance. As such, doctrinal teaching serves as the COMPASS that ensures our students are heading in the right direction in their pursuit of God.

- **C**hanges their focus
- **O**ptimizes their worship
- **M**atures their understanding
- **P**revents their deception
- **A**nswers their questions
- **S**trengthens their witness
- **S**ecures their legacy

There are several different ways doctrine determines the trajectory of our lives, and the acronym helps us understand this truth. Let's explore it together.

Changes Their Focus

The world we live in conditions teens to be self-centered. From social media selfies to individual sports accomplishments, they are taught from an early age that they are the center of the universe. Everything revolves around them. As leaders and parents, we can be guilty of adding fuel to the fire as we attempt to empower them. We frame our encouragement, even our spiritual motivation for them, in selfish terms. We describe God's wonderful plan for their lives, promote a lifestyle that will maximize their happiness, and reassure them of their worth by boosting their self-esteem and focusing on their abilities and achievements.

Sound doctrine shifts the focus from the student in the mirror to the Savior of the universe (Heb 12:2). Directing their attention to the nature of God, his character and attributes, will fill them with amazement while also fostering humility in light of his greatness (Col 3:1–4). Considering the work of his hands will help them find purpose for the work of theirs. Observing his selfless sacrifice for others will inspire their own willingness to give of themselves. As a result, their lives don't have to be lived out of a spiritual perspective that is ultimately self-serving but one that is genuinely motivated by the greatness, grace, and glory of the living God!

Optimizes Their Worship

Sound doctrine will also enable our students to worship "in Spirit and in truth" (John 4:23–24). Too many times students are taught to love and serve God without ever actually learning about who he is. As a result, we can be guilty of worshipping a false idol that is shaped and fashioned by our perceptions of God and who we desire him to be. This results in disappointment and disillusionment as the God our students worship fails to operate based on their expectations. He doesn't work in the ways they expect or deliver what they desire.

Consequently, they find themselves attempting to manufacture sincere love and devotion for a God that doesn't exist, and they don't understand why their hearts aren't satisfied by him. But genuine and passionate affections for God will flow from accurate conceptions of him. And a lifestyle of worship and obedience can only be sustained by an accurate understanding of God, authentic encounters with him, and consistently abiding in his presence.

Matures Their Understanding
Scripture repeatedly instructs us to grow in our knowledge of God (Col 1:10; 2 Pet 3:18). God affirms that it is possible to know and understand him and elevates this personal knowledge as the ultimate priority (Jer 9:23–24). Paul identified knowing him as the loftiest of goals and most noble pursuit (Phil 3:7–8). Yet we neglect introducing some of the more glorious truths about God to teenagers. Sometimes it is because we underestimate their spiritual capacity to learn the deeper truths about God. Other times it is based on our own lack of theological understanding. Perhaps most often it is because we doubt or discount their spiritual appetite for theological truth. But we should teach them to desire the pure milk of the Word so that by it they may grow in respect to their salvation (1 Pet 2:2) in order to mature them to feast on the meatier truths about God (Heb 5:12–6:1).

When we continue to teach familiar stories with surface-level truths, our students will mistakenly believe that they understand all there is to know about God. Their view of God becomes mini-sized and minimized. A deeper knowledge of God will not only provide a stronger foundation for life, but it will also progress them toward maturity in Christ (Col 1:28) and set them on the lifelong path of exploring the inexhaustible depths and unsearchable riches of the wisdom and knowledge of God (Rom 11:33).

Prevents Their Deception
The world is flooding our students' ears and hearts with deceptive voices that are attempting to drown out God's Word and undermine the faith of his young followers. In order to combat these competing philosophies and perspectives, our teenagers must have a solid understanding of what they believe and why they believe it. This will safeguard their hearts from being led astray by the seductive attempts of our culture to convince them that truth is relative, morality is subjective, Scripture is unreliable, and faith is naïve.

The best defense against deception is discipleship. Teaching our students theological truth strengthens their faith as they become rooted and grounded in Scripture (Col 2:7). This safeguards them from drifting in their faith according to the shifting tides of the culture (Heb 2:1) and protects them from being taken captive by the empty and erroneous teachings of the world (Col 2:8).

Answers Their Questions
As students continue to grow, they will experience complicated situations in life that challenge their understanding. Practical issues like family difficulties, personal temptations, and social dynamics, combined with broader life issues such as suffering, death, and injustice, can shake their faith to the core if they aren't equipped to navigate these harsh realities with a biblical understanding. When we fail to teach the deeper and more difficult truths of Scripture, our teens will fail to see any significance for their everyday lives and will question their faith because of the apparent irrelevance of the Bible.

But teaching them theological truth will challenge them to grow beyond the basic understanding of life and will help them face its most difficult experiences with confidence and wisdom. It will also pique their spiritual curiosity as they are introduced to aspects of God's character that extend beyond their elementary exposure. As leaders, we must not attempt to quench this theological thirst with churchy platitudes but must dedicate ourselves to the task of exploring and explaining deeper concepts they long to understand.

Strengthens Their Witness

Our goal in any aspect of discipling students must be to train and equip our students to fulfill the Great Commission (Matt 28:18–20). Scripture challenges all believers to be prepared to make a defense for our faith as we share the eternal hope we have in Christ (1 Pet 3:15). While this does not mean we train our students to become spiritual know-it-alls, it does require us to arm them with the foundational understanding necessary to engage the culture around them.

As they are confronted by skeptics and cynics, and as they encounter a world that is sinfully predisposed to reject the truth, our students must be equipped to withstand the barrage of challenges and critiques they will face. They must be able to contend for the faith (Jude 3) and make the most of every opportunity as they engage the lost world with an informed response for every person and situation (Col 4:5–6).

Secures Their Legacy

Throughout the Old Testament God expressed his intention for his Word to multiply through every generation. Their responsibility to teach their children (Deut 6:4–9) preserved the testimony and legacy of his people and extended his blessing to their offspring (7:12–13). In the same way, our faith will be perpetuated as we train the next generation with biblical truth. In turn, their legacy will be secured as they are equipped to multiply their faith through the succeeding generations.

Therefore, it is critical to provide them with every opportunity to learn and grow in their knowledge and understanding of the Lord. Teaching about his faithfulness, claiming his promises, and obeying his commands provides the foundation necessary to follow and fulfill God's perpetuating strategy. Sound doctrinal teaching not only helps deepen their relationship with Christ, but it also facilitates the spiritual dissemination of truth for the generations to come.

Each of these important outcomes underscores the significance of teaching theology to teenagers. When biblical doctrine is taught effectively to students, it can serve as the COMPASS to help them navigate life's journey and provide reliable direction according to the truth of God's Word. It can also help recalibrate their perspective as they shift their focus to the eternal King and his kingdom, submitting to his authority and following his agenda (Matt 6:33), as they learn to faithfully serve and worship him. As a result, they will become "a good servant of Christ Jesus, nourished by the words of the faith and the good teaching" (1 Tim 4:6).

How Should We Teach Theological Doctrines to Our Students?

Teaching theology and doctrine to students presents a variety of challenges. We have to consider the appropriate time and place for teaching theological truth, as well as the age of our listeners and their present level of knowledge and understanding. Because of the sheer breadth of biblical doctrine, we also have to determine which truths we should prioritize and how to handle some of the more controversial ones. We must also learn to communicate theological truth effectively for teenagers, being mindful of their interest level and their intellectual capacity. In order to effectively accommodate these considerations, we can employ several principles that will enable them to grasp and cling to theological truth.

First, *we must teach them scriptural truth.* The best approach to developing a theological understanding in our students is not through a formal systematic study. We must be committed to teaching theological truth in our regular Bible studies. When we faithfully teach through extended portions of Scripture (i.e., book studies, significant passages, etc.), we must be intentional to identify the theological truths of the text. Every passage, directly or indirectly, teaches us something about who and how God is. Too many times, especially with teenagers, we are so focused on identifying application principles that we fail to expound on the theological truths embedded in the passage.

The theological truths are the foundation and motivation for any practical instruction Scripture teaches. Our students must learn that our obedience is an act of worship in response to the nature and character of God. The best way to introduce students to the majesty and mystery of God is to address the doctrinal truths as we teach expositional Bible studies. When we teach the whole counsel of God (Acts 20:27), theological truth will naturally bubble to the surface and provide the opportunity for us to expound on it.

This approach also helps our students learn how to read and study Scripture in their personal devotions, confirming for them the timeless truths and eternal relevance of the Bible. It also anchors the theological truths we're teaching them in the Word of God so that there is no ambiguity about the source of our understanding or authority. As a result, they learn that our convictions about God must derive from Scripture, not our speculation or opinions.

Second, *we must teach them significant truth.* Similar to medical emergencies where the more serious injuries are treated first, we must perform a sort of "theological triage" that prioritizes the foundational truths of our faith. We can't suffocate our students with theological dogma, inciting doctrinal arguments and debates that aren't healthy or productive (Titus 3:9). Instead, we must focus on the primary and essential doctrines, those that are foundational, non-negotiable, and central to the Christian faith.

The fundamental truths of the faith have intrinsic and infinite worth. But their significance is also found in their relevance. As we disseminate theological truth to our students, we must help them understand how doctrines are crucial to their spiritual walk. Many leaders are fearful that doctrine will drain the life out of their students, boring them and presenting a dull and lifeless Christianity. Yet the opposite is true because doctrinal truth is dynamic truth. Apart from sound doctrine, our understanding of God will be distorted. As a result, our worship will be artificial, our passion will be stifled, and our lives will become futile. Timeless and theological truths stimulate true and vigorous affections for God, prompting and promoting authentic worship and an intimate walk.

The relevance of theological truth also extends into our everyday life. We must teach our students that theological truth is not the same thing as theoretical truth. Theology does not present some idealistic and unrealistic view of the world around us. Instead, it helps us have an accurate understanding that views things from God's perspective. From our routine struggles to life-altering tragedies, and from our everyday blessings to the most meaningful experiences, theology helps us make sense of life. Our students will become enamored with the character and attributes of God when they recognize the practical implications for their lives.

Finally, *we must teach them simple truth*. Deep theological truth does not have to be confusing. As we teach our students the doctrines of the faith, we must aim for clarity and avoid complexity. While theology can require contemplative explanation, we must do our best to communicate in terms that our students can understand. Contemporary examples or illustrations can help "put the cookies on the bottom shelf." This doesn't mean we dilute, distort, or dumb down the truth, but we must make the truth accessible for our listeners.

Jesus often used illustrations to clarify his teachings. He taught soteriology with seeds and soils (Matt 13:1–23). He taught redemption with stories about a lost sheep, a lost coin, and a lost son (Luke 15:1–32). And he taught about eschatology with a fig tree (Mark 13:28–29). Paul also used familiar metaphors throughout his letters to explain the truth. He taught ecclesiology with common body parts like the eyes, ears, and hands (1 Cor 12:12–24). And he explained discipleship using soldiers, athletes, and farmers (2 Tim 2:3–5).

While there are limits to analogies, putting intricate truths in familiar terms can help us engage our students. If we present the truth in a boring fashion or overcomplicate the issues, we will give them the wrong idea about the deeper truths of God. Instead of impressing them with depth, we will frustrate them with confusion. Therefore, we must work hard to communicate theological truth in a relational and relevant way, helping our students become captivated by the immeasurable depths of God's majestic glory.

What Theological Doctrines Should We Teach Our Students?

Pastors and other youth leaders should determine the theological foundation their students should have when they graduate from their ministries. Core doctrines are essential, and secondary doctrines may also be selected based more on the specific demographics of a youth group. While our list is not exhaustive, these are a few of the nonnegotiables every Christian teenager should learn in student ministry.

Doctrine of God

While it seems like a safe assumption that our students would believe in God, it's not a given, especially in today's culture. And with competing religious views swirling around them, an affirmation of God's existence does not automatically equate to Christian orthodoxy. Sadly, the majority of Christian teens are conditioned to view God as their "homeboy" or "the man upstairs." While they may not fully comprehend the intricacies of the Trinity, they should be equipped with a biblical understanding of Christian theism.

The arguments for God. As we teach our students theology, we can't be afraid to raise the questions they will consider privately or be confronted with publicly. While you may choose not to use the philosophical terms, basic arguments for God's existence can help them think intelligently about their faith. The ontological argument (from first cause), the teleological argument (from design or purpose), the cosmological argument (from ultimate existence), and the moral argument (from right/wrong or good/evil) can help them be convinced of God's existence and amazed by God's transcendence.

The authority of God. Our culture conditions our students to reject or resist authority, but the inherent nature of a supreme being implies ultimate authority and our submission to him. But various aspects of God's authority are also necessary for our students to make sense of everything from suffering to salvation. His sovereignty over all of creation affirms his ultimate rule and reign over all of life's circumstances. His power and dominion confirm his ability to perform the impossible—from creating the cosmos to forming a fetus, from shifting the ocean's tides to stirring the human heart, and from working among the nations to answering personal prayers. And his providence assures our students that he is actively involved in their lives and that he is guiding human history toward its ultimate destiny.

The accommodation of God. The concept of divine revelation is critical for students to understand. God has revealed his eternal nature and power through creation as *general revelation* (Rom 1:20). He has also disclosed his personal attributes through two forms of *specific revelation*, the Son and the Scriptures. Jesus is the living Word (John 1:1, 14) who is the physical manifestation of the invisible God (Col 1:15; Heb 1:3) in bodily form (Col 2:9; Phil 2:8). The Bible is the written Word (Heb 4:12) and reveals the character and nature of God as his personal expression (2 Tim 3:16) through divinely inspired authors (2 Pet 1:20–21). It is inerrant (without error in the original manuscripts), inspired (divinely written through human authors), infallible (trustworthy and true), and sufficient (for everything pertaining to life and godliness).

Because God has graciously revealed himself to us in these ways, our students can accurately, though not exhaustively, come to know the only true God (John 17:3). They can grow in their knowledge of him through their personal relationship with Christ (Phil 3:7–8; 2 Pet 3:18) and life-changing encounters through the Scriptures (Heb 4:12). These forms of self-disclosure are God's invitation to know him and will alter the ways our students think about their relationship with God and his Word.

The attributes of God. Through his divine revelation our students can be exposed to the splendor and majesty of God's incomprehensible nature. His transcendent attributes like his omniscience, omnipotence, and omnipresence can inspire their awe and reverence for him. Considering some of his personal characteristics as a holy, righteous, just, merciful, and loving God can enhance their intimacy with him and their imitation of him.

His attributes also include his triune nature as one God (Deut 6:4), existing in the three persons of the Father, the Son, and the Holy Spirit (Matt 28:19; 2 Cor 13:14). The *essential Trinity* affirms the divine essence and intrinsic equality of each individual member, while the *economic Trinity* confirms their specific roles in redemptive history (Eph 1:3–14). Although our students may not completely grasp the complexities of the Godhead, we must affirm for them its reality and its relevance.

Doctrine of Humanity

Our world affirms various things about people that do not reflect the biblical teaching, such as people are fundamentally good, all people are God's children, or that animals are just as valuable as people. This only accentuates the urgent need of teaching our students a scriptural view of humanity. Their view of themselves, others, and the world around them should be determined by what the Bible teaches about people.

Our special nature. The primary doctrinal truth about humanity is our unique nature as the pinnacle of God's creative work. We, unlike any other aspect of his creation, were created in the image of God (Gen 1:26–27). The *imago Dei* includes our intellectual capacity, our moral capacity, and our leadership capacity. But the image of God primarily speaks to our relational capacity. As the members of the Trinity dwell in communion with one another, God has created us in his image to live in fellowship with him. However, Adam's sin separated him from God (Gen 3:8, 23–24), and the relational capacity of humanity was damaged. Now all of humanity bears this consequence of original sin; the image of God has been marred. But, by faith in Christ's substitutionary and sacrificial death for our sin,

117

our relationship with God can be restored (2 Cor 5:18; Col 1:20). As a result, the *imago Dei* is being renewed through the process of sanctification (Rom 8:29; 2 Cor 3:18) until it is completed at our glorification (1 Cor 15:49).

Our sinful nature. Through the original sin of Adam, we have all inherited a sinful nature (Rom 5:12). Prior to salvation we are slaves to this sinful corruption (Rom 6:6), dead in our sin and children under God's wrath (Eph 2:1–3). We possess nothing good within ourselves and can offer nothing of meritorious value to God (Rom 3:10–12). However, in Christ, we are freed from sin and redeemed as his treasured possession (Titus 2:14). Although we still bear the effects of our sinful nature, being enticed by sin in our flesh (Rom 7:14–25), we have the assurance that our salvation is secured by Christ, and by his Spirit we have the power to overcome sin (Rom 8:1–11).

We must teach our students to have a biblical view of humanity because it emphasizes our unique nature and our universal need. They must understand that as bearers of God's image, all people possess equal intrinsic value and inalienable rights, from the unborn to the invalid, including every race, ethnicity, generation, and gender. This also means that all people, as members of the human race, share the same individual need for salvation and reconciliation with God that is only available through Jesus Christ.

Doctrine of Christ
Perhaps the most central of all the core doctrines of the Christian faith is the biblical understanding of Christ. While we may teach our students that Jesus loves them and died for them, and we may recount his teachings and miracles, many times we fail to explain his unique essence or what his death, burial, and resurrection actually accomplished on our behalf.

The person of Christ. The distinguishing mark of orthodox Christianity is the biblical truth regarding the essential nature of Christ. As the second member of the Trinity, Christ is fully God, eternal in nature (John 1:1–3, Phil 2:6), immutable (Heb 13:8), and the sovereign Lord of all creation (Col 1:15–17). He is also fully human, conceived by the Spirit (Luke 1:35), clothed in flesh (John 1:12; Phil 2:7) without surrendering his deity (Col 1:19; 2:9). As the radiance of God's glory, Jesus perfectly reveals God to us (Heb 1:1–3) while also living as a man who perfectly fulfilled the law (Matt 5:17; Heb 4:15). Although students may not fully grasp the hypostatic union, they should affirm its reality, that Jesus is both fully God and fully man. As such, they have a compassionate Savior who can empathize with their struggles (Heb 2:17–18) and a glorious Lord they can worship and obey (Phil 2:9–11).

The work of Christ. Christ's unique essence as both God and man was necessary to uniquely qualify him as the sole mediator between God and humanity (1 Tim 2:5). Only as God could he satisfy the divine wrath against sin, and only as man could he serve as the substitute for humanity. He performed the *work of redemption* as he purchased our salvation with his blood (1 Pet 1:18–19), satisfied the debt of our sin (Col 2:14), and offered us forgiveness for our sins (Eph 1:7; Col 1:14). He accomplished the *work of reconciliation* as he embodied our sin (1 Pet 2:24), suffered God's wrath (1 Pet 3:18), made peace through the blood of his cross (Col 1:20), and restored our relationship with God (2 Cor 5:18–19). Jesus also completed the *work of resurrection* by conquering death, hell, and the grave (1 Cor 15:55–57), triumphing over the enemy (Col 2:15) and rescuing us from the domain of darkness and transferring us into the kingdom of light (Col 1:13; 1 Pet 2:9).

We can be tempted to think that the deeper truths about Christ will make our students lose the simplicity of their faith or the sincerity of their love for him, but their passion for Jesus will actually be enhanced when they are introduced to the magnificence of his nature and the magnitude of his sacrifice.

Our faith in Christ. The person and work of Christ are objective realities that require a personal response. The possibility of a relationship with the divine Messiah and the mercy of salvation and forgiveness cannot simply be affirmed; they must be accepted. Scripture is clear that salvation is received by grace through faith in Christ and cannot be earned (Eph 2:8–9). Genuine faith in Jesus turns from sin and self to trust in the Savior (Acts 2:38; 20:21). Through faith in Christ we are regenerated (Eph 2:4–5), received and sealed with the Holy Spirit (Eph 1:13–14), and are transformed into a new creation (Titus 3:4–6; 2 Cor 5:17). By faith in Christ, we are also adopted as God's children (John 1:12) and are being conformed into the image of his Son (Rom 8:29). As a result of our faith in Christ, our eternity with him in heaven is secured, preserved by him and reserved for us (1 Pet 1:3–5).

This understanding of salvation issues a universal invitation for everyone to be saved (Rom 10:13), but it also identifies Jesus as the exclusive way of salvation (John 14:6; Acts 4:12). Salvation has always been by grace through faith in Christ (see Rom 3:21–26). In the Old Testament it was through faith in the promise of salvation (Messianic prophecies; i.e. Gen 3:15), the picture of salvation (sacrificial system as a shadow of Christ's sacrifice; i.e., Heb 10:1) and by the principle of salvation (justification by faith; i.e., Gen 15:6). Now, through faith in Jesus as the One who has been revealed as the fulfillment of these things, we too can receive salvation (Gal 4:4–6).

We must teach our students about the person and work of Christ in order for them to have a proper understanding of their salvation through faith in him. This teaching also provides them with the urgent motivation to share their faith as they are confronted with the sobering reality of lost people around them and around the world. The impetus for fulfilling the Great Commission will derive from their understanding of the person and work of Christ, the universal availability of the gospel, and the exclusivity of salvation through Christ alone.

Doctrine of the Church

There's no shortage of statistics that document the youth who grow up in church but abandon their spiritual families when they graduate from high school. While there are a lot of contributing factors, one critical missing piece in teenage discipleship is a proper understanding of the church. Sadly, many youth ministry students are never taught to view the church as anything more than a social gathering with a spiritual flare. As a result, few recognize the essence of church membership, its privileges, or its responsibilities.

The church as God's people. The church is the people of God whom Christ ordained with his blessing (Matt 16:18) and obtained with his blood (Acts 20:28). The Bible uses three primary metaphors to characterize the church. As the body of Christ, we are united as God's people through a common faith in our Savior. The concept of the body communicates our collective unity, individual diversity, and practical functionality. As the bride of Christ, we are joined to him in covenant love and have a relationship personified by intimacy and purity (Eph 5:22–33; Rev 21:9). As the building of Christ, we are established on him as the foundation (1 Cor 3:9–11) and the chief cornerstone (1 Pet 2:4–8), stabilized by our union together and serve as the dwelling place for God's presence (Eph 3:19–22).

The church and God's purpose. Christ promised his disciples that he would build his church and establish it on the truth of the great confession (Matt 16:16–18). As God's people, we exist for the purpose of obeying the great commandment, loving God with all of our heart, soul, and mind, and loving others as ourselves (Matt 22:37–40). He also charges us to fulfill the Great Commission by making disciples of all nations, assimilating them into his body, and teaching them to obey his teachings (Matt 28:18–20). We are his witnesses, empowered by the Holy Spirit to carry the gospel into all of the world (Acts 1:8).

We have a responsibility to teach our students that church is more than an extracurricular activity. As believers, teenagers are gifted members of God's chosen people, they get to share in the privileges and promises for God's church, and they are a vital part of a global movement that will impact eternity for the cause of Christ. Shame on us if we fail to help them capture the vision of this reality!

Conclusion

Teaching students theological truth is not an option; it is a necessity. This approach reflects both a high view of Scripture as God's revelation and a high view of students as young and capable disciples. It also demonstrates a core conviction that spiritual growth is predicated on scriptural truth. When we fail to teach our students the foundational truths of the faith, we impede their ability to progress in their relationship with Christ and are guilty of spiritual malnourishment. We also irresponsibly send them into spiritual battle ill equipped to engage the enemy. Tragically we also endorse their defection from the local church by unintentionally misleading them to conclude that God's church and his Word are irrelevant.

By contrast, when we are faithful to educate and equip our students with the theological tenants of the faith, we inspire them to grow deeper in their personal intimacy with Christ. They will become overwhelmed by God's greatness and passionate for his glory. With a theological approach we also prepare them to face the harsh realities of life with an informed perspective and engage a lost world with urgency for the cause of Christ. Teaching sound, biblical truth will also challenge our students to become faithfully committed to God's church, united in his mission, and devoted to continuing Christ's legacy for generations to come.

CONCLUSION

Final Thoughts and First Priorities

S tudent ministry is one of the most rewarding ministries to be a part of because of the radical and immediate transformation that can potentially occur in the lives of teenagers. Younger children don't quite have the spiritual capacity to be effectively discipled, and older adults have complex lives that make drastic transformation more difficult. But, when we establish our student ministries on timeless biblical principles—defining students according to God's perspective, ministering to their immediate family, integrating them into the church, and discipling them through personal mentoring—we have the privilege of witnessing God transform their lives and the trajectory of their futures. A generation can be altered right before our eyes! Praise the Lord for the opportunity he has given us to love, serve, and disciple students!

Because of the potential spiritual impact, the magnitude of responsibility we bear in student ministry deserves and demands a high level of devotion and sacrifice. As a result, many youth pastors experience a personal pressure and spiritual burden few can appreciate. Considering the spiritual responsibility ministry demands, we must prioritize and guard against compromise in two areas of our personal lives.

First, *we must prioritize our personal faith.* It's easy in ministry to focus so much on helping others grow in their faith that we can neglect our own spiritual health. But our personal relationship with Christ deserves our greatest devotion. In Paul's farewell letter to Timothy, he challenged his young pastoral understudy with some important reminders related to his walk with Christ that are relevant for us as well. In Christ we can be confident in our calling (2 Tim 1:9). In Christ we find strength and assurance during difficult seasons in ministry (2 Tim 1:11–12). As a result of our relationship with Christ, we can teach God's Word without wavering as we inspire the faith and love of our students (2 Tim 1:13–14).

From a practical standpoint this means we must guard our devotional time with Christ. While our teaching text and personal reading may overlap, we must make sure to guard our hearts from always reading Scripture with a view toward developing a lesson or Bible study. Also, while we should faithfully pray for our ministries, we must not neglect our own spiritual condition as we commune with our heavenly Father.

The disciplines we are teaching our students must be those which we faithfully practice as well. For example, sharing our faith cannot be limited to an invitation at the end of our teaching. We must be actively witnessing to others by guarding ourselves from becoming insulated from the world within the confines of ministry and frequently looking for opportunities to engage our communities with the gospel. Intimacy with Jesus must always be our highest priority, and we cannot become so busy serving him that we miss the pure joy of abiding in the love of our Savior (Luke 10:38–42).

Second, *we must prioritize our personal family.* Tragically, too many marriages and families have been sacrificed on the altar of ministry. And the unique nature of student ministry makes youth leaders particularly prone to this danger. The late-night events, summers dominated by camps and time away from family, extracurricular activities to attend, and additional time spent outside the typical church office hours can have a cumulating and devastating effect on a youth pastor's home.

In order to guard against some of the cascading impact, we should manage our calendars in a way that preserves time with our families as well as protecting those of our students. We should limit the number of events we schedule each month beyond the typical church times. We should also, when possible, schedule events at times that allow us to be home at a reasonable hour for our children's bedtime. We can also plan family-friendly events that allow our families to participate. While we cannot allow them to distract our students from focusing on spiritual or sensitive issues, involving them in our ministries as much as possible will help them be more understanding when we do have to be gone. It also helps them feel included in the ministry rather than being relegated to secondary support.

We must always remember that our families are our primary ministry. Our ability to lead in the home directly corresponds to our capacity to lead in the church (1 Tim 3:5). And our leadership in the home begins with our devotion to our wives. We must protect our relationship with our brides and not allow ministry and church members to be the only subject of our conversations. We must reserve time for her and emotionally detach from our ministry responsibilities. She is our partner in ministry, and she is our best asset to keep ministry from becoming an idol in our hearts.

Although we may never entertain the thought of being unfaithful, there is a real danger that ministry can become our mistress. Our devotion to the Lord and dedication to our calling should never require us to neglect our wives. In conjunction with our wives, our children must never sense that our students are equally or more important than them. While we should teach our families the sacrifices that serving others can require, we must never become so consumed with our ministries that we disregard our primary responsibility to minister to our own family. In fact, our love and dedication to our families should serve as an example and inspiration for our students and their families.

As we devote ourselves to fulfilling our calling, may God protect our hearts and our homes. May we be diligent to honor our Savior, love our families, guard our testimonies, and serve our students. "Now to him who is able to protect you from stumbling and to make you stand in the presence of his glory, without blemish and with great joy, to the only God our Savior, through Jesus Christ our Lord, be glory, majesty, power, and authority before all time, now and forever. Amen" (Jude 1:24–25).

Name and Subject Index

A

Adams, Jay E.   *100*
adolescence   *19–21*
age-graded   *44–45*

B

Black, David Alan   *19*
Bridges. Jerry   *100*

C

church family   *37–38, 71*
community of faith   *53*
contextualization   *43*

D

delegation   *88–89*
demographic ministry   *37–38, 41*
discipleship   *53, 59–61, 68–70*

E

emerging adults   *19–24*
enlisting volunteers   *82–84*
evangelism   *65–68, 103–104*

F

family   *31–32*
fellowship   *53–54, 56, 70–72*
functions of the church   *39–40, 65, 76–77*

G

generational ministry   *35–36, 42–43*
God's will   *31–33*
great commandment   *40*
Great Commission   *40, 58–61, 110, 121–122*

H

Holy Spirit   *52–53, 99, 122*

I

identity   *24–31*
identity crisis   *7–14*
image of God   *52*
integration   *41–47*

J

justification   *97*

L

Larsen, Eric   *36*
leadership development   *84–87*
leadership recruitment   *82–84*
leadership teams   *47, 88*
logistical support   *81*

M

ministry   *72–74*
ministry conflict   *87*
mission statement   *40–41*

P

parent volunteers   *80–81*

peer pressure   *44–45*

prayer   *100–101*

R

relational support   *81*

relationships   *52, 61–62*

S

sanctification   *96–98, 118*

school   *32–33*

servant leadership   *87, 90*

service   *43, 102–103*

spiritual community   *54, 56–57, 71–72, 85*

spiritual disciplines   *96–98, 100–104, 126*

spiritual formation   *69*

spiritual growth   *46, 95, 97, 121*

spiritual support   *81*

T

target student   *46–47, 84–85, 96*

Tozer, A. W.   *105*

U

unity   *54–58, 71*

V

vision statement   *40–41*

W

worship   *74–75, 103, 107*

Scripture Index

Genesis

1:26–27   *52, 117*
3:8   *117*
3:15   *120*
3:23–24   *117*
9:20–27   *31*
12:1–3   *17*
15:6   *120*
22:5   *75*
35:10–12   *17*
37:2   *22*
37:13   *22*
39:3   *22*
39:7–12   *22*

Exodus

20:12   *31*

Deuteronomy

6:4   *117*
6:4–9   *66, 68, 110*
6:20–25   *66*
7:12–13   *110*

Joshua

1:8   *102*

Judges

4   *17*

1 Samuel

2:18   *23*
2:21   *23*
3:7–14   *23*
3:19   *23*
12:2   *23*
16:7   *11*
17   *17*
17:33   *23*
17:34–37   *23*

2 Samuel

7:8–16   *18*

Esther

2:7   *23*
2:15–18   *23*
4:14   *23*
8:5–17   *23*

Psalms

1:2–3   *102*
19:7–14   *102*

Proverbs

22:6   *66*

Isaiah

1:17   *37*

Jeremiah

9:23–24   *108*

Daniel

1:1–7   *22*

1:8–9   *22*

1:9–16   *22*

1:17–21   *22*

Zechariah

4:6   *98*

Matthew

5:16   *103*

5:17   *119*

6:5–13   *101*

6:33   *111*

7:1–6   *55*

7:7–11   *101*

7:24–27   *101*

8:5–10   *18*

9:36   *61*

9:37–38   *36*

13:1–23   *114*

16:16–18   *121*

16:18   *121*

17:24–27   *23*

20:25–28   *90*

20:26–28   *102*

22:27–40   *39*

22:37–38   *98*

22:37–40   *33, 122*

25:21   *33*

28:18–20   *33, 39, 58, 103,
    110, 122*

28:19   *117*

Mark

1:35   *100*

10:45   *73*

13:28–29   *114*

16:15   *39*

Luke

1:26–38   *18*

1:35   *119*

1:38   *23*

2:46–51   *20*

2:52   *21*

5:16   *100*

6:12   *100*

7:36–50   *18*

8:43–48   *18*

10:38–42   *126*

11:24–26   *28*

13:10–13   *18*

15:1–32   *114*

18:1–8   *101*

19:1–10   *18*

21:2–4   *18*

John

1:1   *116*

1:1–3   *119*

1:12   *26, 119, 120*

1:13   *27*

1:14   *61, 116*
3:3   *27*
3:8   *99*
4:23–24   *103, 107*
9:3   *18*
13:1–17   *102*
13:12–17   *73*
13:35   *32*
14:6   *120*
14:15   *98*
14:16   *99*
14:23   *52*
14:26   *99*
15:5   *98*
15:26   *99*
16:13   *99*
17:3   *26, 116*
17:17   *101*
17:21–23   *56*

Acts
1:8   *103, 122*
2:14–41   *18*
2:38   *65, 120*
2:39   *65*
2:42   *58, 70*
2:42–47   *39*
2:43   *75*
2:44   *71*
2:45   *72*
2:46   *70*
2:46–47   *75*

2:47   *65*
4:12   *120*
4:32   *71*
6:4   *58*
20:21   *120*
20:27   *112*
20:28   *121*
26:4   *23*

Romans
1:16   *103*
1:20   *116*
3:10–12   *118*
3:21–26   *120*
5:8   *98*
5:12   *118*
6:4   *27*
6:6   *118*
6:6–13   *98*
6:11–14   *31*
7:14–25   *118*
7:17   *28*
8   *98*
8:1   *28*
8:1–11   *99, 118*
8:9   *99*
8:11   *28, 99*
8:16   *99*
8:26–27   *99*
8:29   *99, 118, 120*
8:37   *28*
10:13   *120*

11:33	*109*
12:1	*39*
12:1–2	*103, 106*
12:2	*30*
12:10	*32, 73*
13:14	*30*

1 Corinthians

1:10–17	*55*
1:26–31	*12, 18*
2:2	*25*
2:10–16	*99*
3:1–3	*20*
3:9–11	*121*
6:19	*99*
9:24–27	*97*
10:31	*32, 74, 103*
12:12–24	*114*
13:12	*20*
13:13	*71*
15:10	*100*
15:49	*118*
15:55–57	*119*

2 Corinthians

3:18	*99, 118*
5:14	*98*
5:14–15	*39*
5:15	*31*
5:16	*25*
5:17	*25, 27, 29, 120*
5:18	*118*
5:18–19	*119*
5:21	*28*
13:14	*117*

Galatians

2:6	*8*
2:11–16	*18*
3:26–29	*26*
4:4–6	*120*
4:9	*26*
5:18	*99*
5:22–23	*99*
6:2	*72*
6:10	*39, 72*
6:15	*27*

Ephesians

1:3	*28*
1:3–14	*117*
1:7	*119*
1:13–14	*120*
2:1–3	*27, 118*
2:3	*26*
2:4–5	*120*
2:4–10	*27*
2:8	*26*
2:8–9	*120*
2:10	*28*
3:16	*99*
3:19–22	*121*
3:20–21	*24*
4:1	*24*
4:1–6	*71*
4:3	*55*

4:4–5   *52*
4:11–16   *79*
4:22–24   *30*
4:24   *27*
4:29   *32*
5:18   *99*
5:22–33   *121*
6:1   *31*
6:2   *31*
6:4   *68*
6:18   *101*

Philippians
1:27   *56*
2:1   *71*
2:2–3   *32*
2:3–4   *72, 103*
2:5   *9*
2:5–11   *61*
2:6   *119*
2:7   *73, 119*
2:8   *116*
2:9–11   *119*
2:13   *100*
3:3–8   *13*
3:7–8   *108, 116*
3:18   *26*
4:6–7   *101*
4:13   *12, 98*

Colossians
1:10   *108*
1:13   *119*

1:14   *119*
1:15   *116*
1:15–17   *119*
1:19   *119*
1:19–20   *52*
1:20   *26, 118, 119*
1:21   *26*
1:21–22   *27*
1:28   *109*
1:28–29   *21, 39*
2:3   *28*
2:7   *109*
2:8   *109*
2:9   *116, 119*
2:14   *119*
2:15   *119*
3:1–4   *107*
3:3–10   *30*
3:10   *27*
3:16   *75, 103*
3:17   *32*
3:20   *31*
3:23   *32*
4:2–6   *103*
4:3–6   *39, 67*
4:5–6   *110*

1 Thessalonians
2:8   *39, 59, 69*
2:19–20   *xv*
5:14   *87*
5:17   *101*
5:18   *32*

2 Thessalonians

3:7–9   *60*

1 Timothy

2:1   *101*

2:2   *43*

2:5   *119*

3:5   *127*

4:6   *111*

4:7   *97*

4:7–8   *33*

4:12   *23, 24*

5   *37*

5:3–16   *38*

5:9   *38*

2 Timothy

1:9   *126*

1:11–12   *126*

1:13–14   *126*

2:2   *39, 58, 70*

2:3–5   *114*

2:3–6   *97*

2:15   *102*

2:22   *23, 38*

2:22–23   *54*

3:15   *101*

3:16   *101, 116*

Titus

2   *42*

2:2–8   *20*

2:11–12   *30*

2:11–14   *38, 99*

2:14   *118*

3:3–7   *28*

3:4–6   *120*

3:5   *27*

3:9   *113*

Hebrews

1:1–3   *119*

1:3   *116*

2:1   *109*

2:17–18   *119*

4:12   *101, 116*

4:14–16   *101*

4:15   *119*

5:12–6:1 *20, 108*

10:1   *120*

10:24–25 *32, 53, 71*

12:2   *107*

12:6   *96*

12:11   *97*

13:8   *119*

13:15   *103*

James

1:22–25   *102*

1:25   *102*

1:27   *37*

2:1–9   *55*

3:1   *82*

4:1–2   *54*

5:16   *101*

1 Peter

1:3   *27*

1:3–5   *120*

1:13–16   *97*

1:14–16   *30*

1:18–19   *119*

1:23   *27, 101*

2:2   *101, 108*

2:4–8   *121*

2:9   *26, 119*

2:24   *119*

3:15   *110*

3:15–16   *103*

3:18   *119*

4:2–4   *30*

5:7   *101*

2 Peter

1:20–21   *116*

3:18   *108, 116*

1 John

1:3   *39*

1:6–7   *71*

1:7   *53*

2:12–14   *19, 37*

3:1   *26, 28*

4:10   *98*

5:3   *98*

3 John

4   *104*

Jude

1:24–25   *128*

3   *110*

Revelation

21:9   *121*